THE DANITES:

AND

OTHER CHOICE SELECTIONS

FROM THE WRITINGS OF

JOAQUIN MILLER,

"THE POET OF THE SIERRAS."

"A little bird
From bunch of grass flew sudden out,
And swinging circled sharp about,
Then tangled in a spangled tree,
And there, as if the whole world heard,
Began its morning minstrelsy."
—THE BARONESS.

EDITED BY
A. V. D. HONEYMAN.

NEW YORK:
THE AMERICAN NEWS COMPANY,
1878.

HONEYMAN & ROWE,
Steam Printers,
Somerville, N. J.

SMITH & McDOUGAL,
Electrotypers,
82 Beekman St., N. Y.

Dedicated

TO ALL WHO ADMIRE,

EVEN TO THE HUMBLEST EXTENT,

THE WRITINGS OF

JOAQUIN MILLER.

Her mouth was Egypt's mouth of old
Pushed out and pouting full and bold
With simple beauty. Why her mouth
Was roses gathered from the South—
The warm South side of Paradise
And breathed upon and banded down
By angels on a stair of stars.

Joaquin Miller

PREFACE.

BELIEVING sincerely that "the gardens of God"—and I speak reverently, meaning His gardens in the human soul, where is grown whatever is most lovely in this world—in their yield of *flowers of song* have rarely given such fruitage as the poems of the "wild songster of Oregon," I send forth this volume of choice selections from JOAQUIN MILLER's prose and verse. They are choice in the sense that they are Mr. MILLER's best, so far as the editor's judgment could determine, although others equally marked in their beauty or originality have been omitted. To choose a sufficient number for these pages has been as little a task, indeed, as to pluck a handful of roses among a thousand varieties in the King's Park!

I am aware of the merciless denunciation of this author's verse at the hands of a few American writers of "book notices." But time may prove the first convictions of the best English reviewers to be correct. The London critics are not usually caught napping! Let the present generation in America die, and the next will admit that the cross of song may be planted upon the Sierras as well as the Alps or the Catskills, and that Genius has no territorial limitations save that of the most ultimate rim of the universe of God.

What is true poetry? In one of Mr. MILLER's lectures it is defined as a succession of beautiful pictures, whether in prose or verse. If this be correct—and is it not?—where in all American verse can you find more luxuriance of imagination, more wealth of imagery, than in, for instance, *The Songs of the Sunlands?* And his prose is nearly as full of suggestive figures, while as simple and peaceful as the talks of the Red Man, who was his earliest friend and teacher.

The poet has a great, warm heart, and his songs are invariably for Peace and Charity. Some of the "Olive Leaves," gathered in *The Songs of the Sunlands*, will be found to be as echoes of that choir which sang, over Bethlehem's plains, "Peace on earth, good will to men."

But let every one be his own judge, whether or not this new singer of the New World is entitled to the fame which would seem to be already secure. This book will give him the opportunity in the most compact space possible.

The approval of Mr. MILLER has been secured for this selected work, but he is not personally responsible for its suggestion, arrangement, nor publication. Neither the selections, nor their titles,* nor the accompanying notes respecting the different books from which extracts are taken, have passed his eye: he has confided to the editor's judgment. Accordingly, it has not been deemed wise, thus apart from his revision, to make even the slightest verbal corrections of some rhetorical faults.

The italic excerpts on pages fronting the book-titles are all from the same author, with the exception of the last.

That the pure, sweet melody of these Western bird-notes, the fresh, woodland fragrance of these flowers of the Pacific coast, may appeal to other hearts as they have to mine, and affect them as sensibly for *good*, is my earnest wish.

A. V. D. H.

SOMERVILLE, N. J., *Nov.* 16, 1877.

---

* In all but rare instances the titles have been supplied by the editor, the selections being from long poems.

CONTENTS.

Songs of the Sunlands.

Unwritten History; or, Life Amongst the Modocs.

The Ship in the Desert.

The Baroness of New York.

THE DANITES,

AND

THE FIRST FAM'LIES OF THE SIERRAS.

THOSE who have read "The First Fam'lies of the Sierras," and have also witnessed the drama of "The Danites," will at once recognize the nearly perfect likeness. They are, indeed, one; the latter being simply the former adapted to the stage. In making the selections which follow under this title, the editor has drawn from both the drama and the book.

"The First Fam'lies" is a semi-autobiography, like "Unwritten History," and "The One Fair Woman," although it may take a keener eye to detect the real amid the ideal. As a specimen of California vernacular, and a delineator of life in the mining camps, it is probably not exceeded by any of the famed works of BRET HARTE, although its publication attracted less attention than *The Luck of Roaring Camp*, or *The Outcasts of Poker Flat.* It was partially written in California, but completed in London in 1874, where it was published by George Rutledge. In this country its publishers are Jansen, McClurg & Co., Chicago, 1876.

"The Danites" took its name from those Mormons who were banded together as "Avenging Angels," and pursued after "the lost Nancy Williams," the last of the persecuted family of that name, so well known to Mormon history. The death of Brigham Young having revived the story, additional interest is lent to what will doubtless prove one of the most successful dramas lately put upon the stage.

Is it worth while that we battle to humble
Some poor fellow-soldier down into the dust?
God pity us all! Time eftsoon will tumble
All of us together like leaves in a gust,
Humbled indeed down into the dust.

Little Billy Piper.

"WHAT is your name, my boy?"

"Billy Piper."

The timid brown eyes looked up through the cluster of yellow curls, as the boy stepped aside to let the big man pass; and the two, without other words, went on their ways.

Oddly enough they allowed this boy to keep his name. They called him Little Billy Piper. He was an enigma to the miners. Sometimes he looked to be only fifteen. Then again he was very thoughtful. The fair brow was wrinkled sometimes; there were lines, sabre cuts of time, on the fair delicate face, and then he looked to be double that age.

He worked, or at least he went out to work, every day with his pick and pan and shovel; but almost always they saw him standing by the running stream, looking into the water, dreaming, seeing in Nature's mirror the snowy clouds that blew in moving mosaic overhead and through and over the tops of the tossing firs.

He rarely spoke to the men more than in monosyllables. Yet when he did speak to them his language was so refined, so far above their common speech, and his voice was so soft, and his manner so gentle, that they saw in him a superior.

A Question.

"TELL me," said the boy, laying his hand on the arm of his companion, and looking earnestly and sadly in his face, "Tell me, Tim, why it is that they always have the grave-yard on a hill. Is it because it is a little nearer to heaven?" His companion did not understand. And yet he did understand, and was silent.

King Sandy.

THIS Sandy never blustered or asserted himself at all. He was born above most men of his class, and he stood at their head boldly without knowing it. Had he been born an Indian he would have been a chief, would have led in battle, and dictated in council, without question or without opposition from any one. Had he been born in the old time of kings, he would have put out his hand, taken a crown, and worn it as a man wears the most fitting garment, by instinct. Sandy was born king of the Forks. He was king already, without knowing it or caring to rule it.

There are people just like that in the world, you know,—great, silent, fearless fellows, or at least there are in the Sierra-world, and they are as good as they are great. They are there, throned there, filling up more of the world than any ten thousand of those feeble things that God sent into the world, in mercy to the poor good men who sit all day silent, and cross-legged, and in nine parts, sewing, on a table.

They will not go higher, they cannot go lower. They accept the authority as if they had inherited through a thousand sires.

Limber Tim.

Now there was Limber Tim, one of the first and best men of all the thousand bearded and brawny set of Missourians, a nervous, weakly, sensitive sort of a fellow, who kept always twisting his legs and arms around as he walked, or talked, or tried to sit still; who never could face anything or any one two minutes without flopping over, or turning around, or twisting about, or trying to turn himself wrong side out, and of course anybody instinctively knew his name as soon as he saw him.

The baptismal name of Limber Tim was Thomas Adolphus Grosvenor. And yet these hairy, half-savage, unread Missourians, who had stopped here in their great pilgrimage of the plains, and had never yet seen a city, or the sea, or a school-house, or a church, knew perfectly well that there was a mistake in this matter the moment they saw him, and that his name was Limber Tim.

Bunker Hill.

ONE day, Bunker Hill, a humped-back and unhappy woman of uncertain ways, passed through the crowd in The Forks. Some of the rough men laughed and made remarks. This boy was there also. Lifting his eyes to one of these men at his side, he said:

"God has made some women a little plain, in order that he might have some women that are wholly good."

The Miners' Wash-day.

BRAWNY-MUSCLED men, nude above the waist, "naked and yet not ashamed," hairy-breasted and bearded, noble, kingly men — miners washing their shirts in a mountain-stream of the Sierras. Thoughtful, earnest, splendid men! Boughs above them, pine-tops toying with the sun that here and there reached through like fingers pointing at them from the far, pure purple of the sky. And a stillness so profound, perfect, holy as a temple! Nature knows her Sabbath.

I would give more for a painting of this scene—that sun, that sky and wood, the water there, the brave, strong men, the thinkers and the workers there, nude and natural, silent and sincere, bending to their work—than for all the battle-scenes that could be hung upon a palace wall. When the great man comes, the painter of the true and great, these men will be remembered.

Washee-Washee.

THERE was an expression of ineffable peace and tranquility on the face of Washee-Washee that twilight, as he wended his way from the Widow's cabin to his own. His day's work was done; and the little man's face looked the soul of repose. Possibly he was saying with the great, good poet, whose lines you hear at evening time, on the lips of nearly every English artisan—

> "Something attempted, something done,
> Has earn'd a night's repose."

Washee-Washee looked strangely fat for a Chinaman, as he peacefully toddled down the trail, still wearing, as he neared his cabin, that look of calm delight and perfect innocence, such only as the pure in heart are supposed to wear. His hands were drawn up and folded calmly across his obtruding stomach, as if he feared he might possibly burst open, and wanted to be ready to hold himself together.

In the great-little republic there, where all had begun an even and equal race in the battle of life, where all had begun as beggars, this tawny little man from the far-off Flowery Kingdom was alone; he was the only representative of his innumerable millions in all that camp. And he did seem so fat, so perfectly full of satisfaction. Perhaps he smiled to think how fat he was, and, too, how he had flourished in the little democracy.

He was making a short turn in the trail, still holding his clasped hands over his extended stomach, still smiling peacefully out of his half-shut eyes:

"Washee! Washee!"

A double bolt of thunder was in his ears. A tremendous hand reached out from behind a pine, and then the fat little Chinaman squatted down and began to wilt and melt beneath it.

"Washee-Washee, come!"

Washee-Washee was not at all willing to come; but that made not the slightest difference in the world to Sandy. The little almond-eyed man was not at all heavy. Old flannel shirts, cotton overalls, stockings, cotton collars and cambric handkerchiefs never are heavy, no matter how well they may be wadded in, and padded away, and tucked up, and twisted under an outer garment; and so before he had time to say a word he was on his way to the Widow's with Sandy, while Limber Tim, with his mouth half open, came cork-screwing up the trail, and grinding and whetting his screechy gum boots together after them.

He reached the door of the Widow's cabin, knocked with the knuckles of his left hand, while his right hand held on to an ankle that hung down over his left shoulder, and calmly waited an answer. The door half way opened.

"Beg pardon, mum."

He bowed stiffly as he said this, and then shifting Washee-Washee around, quietly took his other heel in his other hand, and proceeded to shake him up and down, and dance him and stand him gently on his head, until the clothes began to burst out from under his blue seamless garment, and to peep through his pockets, and to reach down around his throat and dangle about his face, till the little man was nearly smothered.

Then Sandy set him down a moment to rest, and he looked in his face as he sat there, and it had the same peaceful smile, the same calm satisfaction as before.

The little man now put his head to one side, shut

his pretty brown eyes a little tighter at the corners, and opened his mouth the least bit in the world, and put out his tongue as if he was about to sing a hymn.

Then Sandy took him up again. He smiled sweeter than before. Sandy tilted him sidewise, and shook him again. Then there fell a spoon, then a pepper-box, and then a small brass candlestick; and at last, as he rolled him over and shook the other side, there came out a machine strangely and wonderfully made of whalebone and brass, and hooks and eyes, that Sandy had never seen before, and did not at all understand, but supposed was either a fish-trap or some new invention for washing gold.

Then Limber Tim, who had screwed his back up against the pailings, and watched all this with his mouth open, came down, and reaching out with his thumb and finger, as if they had been a pair of tongs, took the garments one by one, named them, for he knew them and their owners well, and laid them silently aside. Then he took Washee-Washee from the hands of Sandy and stood him up, or tried to stand him up alone. He looked like a flag-staff, with the banner falling loosely around it in an indolent wind. He held him up by the queue awhile, but he wilted and sank down gently at his feet, all the time smiling sweetly as before; all the time looking up with a half-closed eye and half-parted lips, as though he was enjoying himself perfectly, and would like to laugh, only that he had too much respect for the present company.

Washee-Washee Sentenced.

They marched Washee-Washee to the Howling Wilderness, told the sentence, and called upon the Parson to enforce judgment. He now took a cordial and began. Washee-Washee sat before him on a bench, leaning against the wall. The little man seemed as if he was about to go to sleep; possibly his conscience had kept him awake the night before, when he found that all his little investments had been a failure in the Forks.

The Parson began. Washee-Washee flinched, jerked back, sat bolt upright, and seemed to suffer. Then the Parson shot another oath. This time it came like a cannon-ball, and red-hot, too, for Washee-Washee was almost lifted out of his seat.

Then the Parson took his breath a bit, rolled the quid of tobacco in his mouth from left to right and from right to left, and as he did so he selected the very broadest, knottiest, and ugliest oaths that he had found in all his fifty years of life at sea and on the border.

Washee-Washee had lost his expression of peace. He had evidently been terribly shaken. The Parson had rested a good spell, however, and the little, slim, brown man before him, who had crawled out over the Great Wall of China, sailed across the sea of seas, climbed the Sierras, and sat down in their midst to begin the old clothes business, without pay or promise, was again settling back, as if about to surrender to sleep. Cannon balls! conical shot! chain shot! and shot red-hot! Never were such oaths heard in the world before! The Chinaman fell over.

"Stop!" cried the bar-keeper of the Howling Wilderness, who didn't want the expense of the funeral; "stop! do you mean to cuss him to death?"

The Chinaman was allowed time to recover, and then they sat him again on the bench. A man fanned him with his broad bamboo hat, lest he should faint before the last half of the punishment was nearly through, and the Judge was called upon to enforce the remainder of their sentence. The Judge came forward slowly, put his two hands back under his coat tails, tilted forward on his toes and began:

"Washee-Washee! In this glorious climate of Californy—how could you?"

Washee-Washee nodded, and the Judge broke down

badly embarrassed. At last he recovered himself, and began in a deep, earnest and entreating tone:

"Washee-Washee, in this glorious climate of Californy, you should remember the seventh commandment, and never, under any circumstances or temptations that beset you, should you covet your neighbor's goods, or his boots, or his shirts, or his socks, or his handkerchief, or anything that is his, or——"

The Judge paused, the men giggled, and then they roared, and laughed, and danced about their little Judge; for Washee-Washee had folded his little brown hands in his lap, and was sleeping as sweetly as a baby in its cradle.

A Pure Woman.

She is pure—a pure, good woman. Do you see the snow that mantles yonder mountain, kissed by the clouds and the morning sun, and speckless as the lily's inmost leaf? 'Tis not more pure than she.

Some Men's Characters.

Some men are with their characters much as they are with their money; the less they have the more careful they have to be.*

* A few other selections will be found among the "Miscellanies" at the close of this volume.

SONGS OF THE SIERRAS.

THE first volume of MILLER's poems, with the above title, was published in May, 1871, by Longmans & Son, London, Eng., and a few months later by Roberts Bros., Boston. It consists of ten poems. The first, "Arizonian," perhaps as poetical as any, was mostly written in London under an odd circumstance. The author was invited by Mr. Spurgeon to hear him preach upon a certain day. MILLER's wardrobe being scanty, he ordered new clothes and boots for the occasion. Neither fitted him. The latter were especially annoying, and, while vainly trying to put them on, the composition forced itself into audible words,—

> And I have said, and I say it ever,
> As the years go on and the world goes over,
> 'Twere better to be content and clever;'"

and when he gave up the task in despair, instead of hearing Spurgeon he wrote "Arizonian," with these as the opening lines. "Californian" is the oldest poem, written in California, and first called "Joaquin." "Ina" was called "Oregonian" in the English edition—changed because the book was ill received in Oregon. Its characters are from life, being two well-known authors. "The Tale of the Tall Alcalde" is largely autobiography. It, and "Myrrh," and also "Even So," were mostly written in California. "Burns and Byron" were composed at Nottingham. Upon the appearance of this single work MILLER ascended to the pinnacle of fame in England.

Because the skies were blue, because
The sun in fringes of the sea
Was tangled, and delightfully
Kept dancing on as in a waltz,
And tropic trees bow'd to the seas,
And bloom'd and bore, years through and through,
And birds in blended gold and blue
Were thick and sweet as swarming bees,
And sang as if in Paradise,
And all that Paradise was Spring—
Did I too sing with lifted eyes,
Because I could not choose but sing.

A Storm on the River.

I LAY in my hammock; the air was heavy
And hot and threat'ning; the very heaven
Was holding its breath; and bees in a bevy
Hid under my thatch; and birds were driven
In clouds to the rocks in a hurried whirr
As I peer'd down by the path for her.
She stood like a bronze bent over the river,
The proud eyes fixed, the passion unspoken—
When the heavens broke like a great dyke broken.
Then, ere I fairly had time to give her
A shout of warning, a rushing of wind
And the rolling of clouds and a deafening din
And a darkness that had been black to the blind
Came down, as I shouted, "Come in! come in!
Come under the roof, come up from the river,
As up from a grave—come now, or come never!"
The tassel'd tops of the pines were as weeds,
The red-woods rock'd like to lake-side reeds,
And the world seem'd darken'd and drown'd forever.

In the Tropics.

Birds hung and swung, green-robed and red,
Or droop'd in curved lines dreamily,
Rainbows reversed, from tree to tree,
Or sang low, hanging overhead—
Sang low, as if they sang and slept;
Sang faint, like some far waterfall,
And took no note of us at all,
Though nuts that in the way were spread
Did crush and crackle as we stept.
Wild lilies, tall as maidens are,
As sweet of breath, as pearly fair,

As fair as faith, as pure as truth,
Fell thick before our every tread,
As in a sacrifice to ruth,
And all the air with perfume fill'd
More sweet than ever man distill'd.
There came the sweet song of sweet bees,
With chorus-tones of cockatoo,
That slid his beak along the bough,
And walk'd and talk'd and hung and swung,
In crown of gold and coat of blue,
The wisest fool that ever sung,
Or had a crown, or held a tongue.
How wild and still with wonder stood
The proud mustangs with banner'd mane,
And necks that never knew a rein,
And nostrils lifted high, and blown,
Fierce breathing as a hurricane.

The Bleeding Past.

O PASSION-TOSSED and bleeding past!
Part now, part well, part wide apart,
As ever ships on ocean slid
Down, down the sea, hull, sail and mast.

Drowned.

DEEDS strangle memories of deeds,
And blossoms wither, choked with weeds,
And floods drown memories of men.

The Warm Sea's Dimpled Face.

THE warm sea laid his dimpled face,
With every white hair smoothed in place,
As if asleep against the land.

Loves of the Sun-Maids.

No lands where any ices are
Approach, or ever dare compare
With warm loves born beneath the sun.
The one the cold white steady star,
The lifted shifting sun the one.
I grant you fond, I grant you fair,
I grant you honor, trust and truth,
And years as beautiful as youth,
And many years beyond the sun,
And faith as fixed as any star;
But all the North-land hath not one
So warm of soul as sun-maids are.

Death of a Warrior.

A bow, a touch of heart, a pall
Of purple smoke, a crash, a thud,
A warrior's raiment rent, and blood,
A face in dust and—that was all.

Walker in Nicaragua.

A piercing eye, a princely air,
A presence like a chevalier,
Half angel and half Lucifer;
Fair fingers, jewell'd manifold
With great gems set in hoops of gold;
Sombrèro black, with plume of snow
That swept his long silk locks below;
A red serape with bars of gold,
Heedless falling, fold on fold;
A sash of silk, where flashing swung
A sword as swift as serpent's tongue,
In sheath of silver chased in gold;

A face of blended pride and pain,
Of mingled pleading and disdain,
With shades of glory and of grief;
And Spanish spurs with bells of steel
That dash'd and dangl'd at the heel—
The famous fillibuster chief
Stood by his tent 'mid tall brown trees
That top the fierce Cordilleras,
With brawn arm arched above his brow;—
Stood still—he stands, a picture, now—
Long gazing down the sunset seas.

Prophecy of the West.

DARED I but say a prophecy,
As sang the holy men of old,
Of rock-built cities yet to be
Along these shining shores of gold,
Crowding athirst into the sea,
What wondrous marvels might be told!
Enough, to know that empire here
Shall burn her loftiest, brightest star;
Here art and eloquence shall reign,
As o'er the wolf-rear'd realm of old;
Here learned and famous from afar,
To pay their noble court, shall come,
And shall not seek, or see in vain,
But look on all with wonder dumb.

After the Battle.

SOME skulls that crumble to the touch,
Some joints of thin and chalk-like bone,
A tall black chimney, all alone,
That leans as if upon a crutch,
Alone are left to mark or tell,
Instead of cross or cryptic stone,
Where fair maids loved, or brave men fell.

Walker's Grave.

I LAY this crude wreath on his dust,
Inwove with sad, sweet memories
Recalled here by these colder seas.
I leave the wild bird with his trust,
To sing and say him nothing wrong;
I wake no rivalry of song.
No sod, no sign, no cross nor stone,
But at his side a cactus green
Upheld its lances long and keen;
It stood in hot red sands alone,
Flat-palm'd and fierce with lifted spears;
One bloom of crimson crown'd its head,
A drop of blood, so bright, so red,
Yet redolent as roses' tears.
In my left hand I held a shell,
All rosy-lipp'd and pearly red;
I laid it by his lowly bed,
For he did love so passing well
The grand songs of the solemn sea.
O shell! sing well, wild, with a will,
When storms blow loud and birds be still,
The wildest sea-song known to thee!

The Sierras.

AFAR the bright Sierras lie
A swaying line of snowy white,
A fringe of heaven hung in sight
Against the blue base of the sky.

The Sun on the Sierras.

THE day-star dances on the snow
That gleams along Sierra's crown
In gorgeous, everlasting glow,
And frozen glory and renown.

The Upturned Face.

An upturned face so sweetly fair,
So sadly, saintly, purely fair,
So rich of blessedness and bliss!
I know she is not flesh and blood,
But some sweet spirit of this wood;
I know it by her wealth of hair,
And step on the unyielding air;
Her seamless robe of shining white,
Her soul-deep eyes of darkest night:
But over all and more than all
That could be said or can befall,
That tongue can tell or pen can trace,
That wondrous witchery of face.

Curambo's Fear of Death.

Oh! for the rest—for the rest eternal!
Oh! for the deep and the dreamless sleep!
Where never a hope lures to deceive;
Where never a heart beats but to grieve;
Nor thoughts of heaven or hells infernal,
Shall ever wake or dare to break
The rest of an everlasting sleep!
Is there truth in the life eternal?
Will our memories never die?
Shall we relive in realms supernal
Life's resplendent and glorious lie!
Death has not one shape so frightful
But defiantly I would brave it;
Earth has nothing so delightful
But my soul would scorn to crave it,
Could I know for sure, for certain,
That the falling of the curtain
And the folding of the hands
Is the full and the final casting
Of accounts for the everlasting!
Everlasting and everlasting!

Love in the Cycled Years.

AWAY to where the orange tree
Is white through all the cycled years,
And love lives an eternity;
Where birds are never out of tune
And life knows no decline of noon;
Where winds are sweet as woman's breath,
And purpled, dreamy, mellow skies
Are lovely as a woman's eyes,—
There we in calm and perfect bliss
Of boundless faith and sweet delight
Shall realize the world above,
Forgetting all the wrongs of this,
Forgetting all of blood and death,
And all your terrors of to-night,
In pure devotion and deep love.

Into the Flame.

AGAIN she lifts her brown arms bare,
Far flashing in their bands of gold
And precious stones, rare, rich, and old.
Was ever mortal half so fair?
Was ever such a wealth of hair?
Was ever such a plaintive air?
Was ever such a sweet despair?

Still humbler now her form she bends;
Still higher now the flame ascends:
She bares her bosom to the sun.
Again her jewell'd fingers run
In signs and sacred form and prayer.
She bows with awe and holy air
In lowly worship to the sun;
Then, rising, calls her lover's name,
And leaps into the leaping flame.

I do not hear the faintest moan,
Or sound, or syllable, or tone.
The red flames stoop a moment down,
As if to raise her from the ground;
They whirl, they swirl, they sweep around
With lightning feet and fiery crown;
Then stand up tall, tip-toed, as one
Would hand a soul up to the sun!

The Morning.

THE day-king hurls a dart
At darkness, and his cold black heart
Is pierced; and now, compelled to flee,
Flies bleeding to the farther sea.

The Chieftain's Form.

HIS breast was like a gate of brass,
His brow was like a gathered storm;
There is no chisell'd stone that has
So stately and complete a form,
In sinew, arm, and every part,
In all the galleries of art.

Popocatapetl.

POPOCATAPETL looms lone like an island
Above the white cloud-waves that break up against him;
Around him white buttes in the moonlight are flashing
Like silver tents pitch'd in the fields of heaven;
While standing in line in their snows everlasting,
Flash peaks, as my eyes into heaven are lifted,
Like milestones that lead to the city eternal.

The Indian Warrior's Address.

ONCE like pines around a mountain
Did my braves in council stand;
Now I call you loud like thunder,
And you come at my command
Faint and few, with feeble hand.

Lo! our daughters have been gathered
From among us by the foe,
Like the lilies they once gather'd
In the spring-time all aglow
From the banks of living snow.

Through the land where we for ages
Laid the bravest, dearest dead,
Grinds the savage white man's ploughshare,
Grinding sires' bones for bread—
We shall give them blood instead.

I saw white skulls in a furrow,
And around the cursèd share
Clung the flesh of my own children
And my mother's tangled hair
Trail'd along the furrow there.

O, my mother up in cloud-land!
(Long arms lifting like the spray)
Whet the flint-heads in my arrows,
Make my heart as hard as they,
Nerve me like a bear at bay!

Warriors! braves! I cry for vengeance!
And the dim ghosts of the dead
Unavenged, do wail and shiver
In the storm-cloud overhead,
And shoot arrows battle-red.

Then he ceased, and sat among them,
With his long locks backward strown,
They as mute as men of marble,
He a king upon a throne,
And as still as polish'd stone.

The Sunset.

A FLUSHED and weary messenger a-west
Is standing at the half-closed door of day,
As he would say, "Good night;" and now his bright
Red cap he tips to me and turns his face.
Were it an unholy thing to say, an angel
Beside the door stood with uplifted seal?
Behold the door seal'd with that blood-red seal
Now burning, spreading o'er the mighty West.

The Night.

THE tawny, solemn Night, child of the East,
Her mournful robes trails on the distant woods,
And comes this way with firm and stately step.
Afront, and very high, she wears her shining
Breast-plate of silver, and on her dark brow
The radiant Venus burns like flashing wit.
Behold! how in her gorgeous flow of hair
Glitter a million mellow-yellow gems,
Spilling their molten gold on the dewy grass.
Throned on the boundless plain, and gazing down
Calmly upon the red-seal'd tomb of day,
Resting her form against the Rocky Mountains,
She rules with silent power a peaceful world.

'Tis midnight now. The bent and broken moon,
Battered and black, as from a thousand battles,
Hangs silent on the purple walls of heaven;

The angel warrior, guard of the gates eternal,
In battle-harness girt, sleeps on the field;
But when to-morrow comes, when wicked men
That fret the patient earth are all astir,
He will resume his shield, and, facing earthward,
The gates of heaven guard from sins of earth.

Don Carlos' Hyperbole.

OH! I would give the green leaves of my life
For something grand and real—undream'd deeds!
To wear a mantle, broad and richly jewell'd
As purple heaven fringed with gold at sunset;
To wear a crown as dazzling as the sun,
And, holding up a sceptre, lightning-charged,
Stride out among the stars as I have strode
A bare-foot boy among the butter-cups.
I'd build a pyramid of the whitest skulls,
And step therefrom unto the spotted moon,
And thence to stars, thence to the central suns;
Then with one grand and mighty leap would land
Unhinder'd on the shores of the gods of old,
And, sword in hand, unbared and unabash'd,
Would stand forth in the presence of the God
Of gods; there, on the jewell'd inner-side
The walls of heaven, carve with a Damascus
Steel, highest up, a grand and titled name
That time nor tide could touch or tarnish ever.
Yea, anything on earth, in hell, or heaven,
Rather than lie a nameless clod forgot,
Letting stern Time in triumph forward tramp
Above my tombless and neglected dust.

Night and Morning in Oregon.

AT night, o'erspread by the rich, purple robe,
The deep imperial Tyrian hue that folds

The invisible form of the Eternal God,
You will see the sentry stars come marching forth
And take their posts upon the field above,
Around the great white tent where sleeps their chief;
You will hear the kakea singing in a dream
The wildest, sweetest song a soul can drink.
And when the tent is folded up, and all
The golden-fringed red sentries face about
To let the pompous day-king pass along,
We too will stand upon a sloping hill,
Where white-lipped springs come leaping, laughing up
With water spouting forth in merry song
Like bridled mirth from out a school-girl's throat,
And look far down the bending Willamette,
And in his thousand graceful curves and strokes
And strange meanderings men misunderstand,
Read the unutterable name of God.

To be a Poet.

It is to want a friend, to want a home,
A country, money—ay, to want a meal.
It is not wise to be a poet now,
For the world has so fine and modest grown,
It will not praise a poet to his face,
But waits till he is dead some hundred years,
Then uprears marbles cold and stupid as itself.

Nature in Unrest.

What! Nature quiet, peaceful, uncomplaining?
I've seen her fretted like a lion caged,
Chafe like a peevish woman cross'd and churl'd,
Tramping and foaming like a whelpless bear;
Have seen her weep, till earth was wet with tears,
Then turn all smiles,—a jade that won her point;
Have seen her tear the hoary hair of Ocean,

While he, himself, full half a world, would moan
And roll and toss his clumsy hands all day,
To earth, like some great helpless babe, that lay
Rude-rock'd and cradled by an unseen nurse,
Then stain her snowy hem with salt-sea tears.

Longings.

Oh! for the skies of rolling blue,
The balmy hours when lovers woo,
When the moon is doubled as in desire,
The dreamy call of the cockatoo
From the orange snow in his crest of fire,
Like vespers calling the soul to bliss!
In the blessed love of the life above,
Ere it has taken the stains of this.

The Valley.

An unkissed virgin at my feet,
Lay my pure, hallow'd, dreamy vale,
Where breathed the essence of my tale—
Lone dimpled in the mountain's face,
Lone Eden in a boundless waste—
It lay so beautiful! so sweet!

The Stream.

It was unlike all other streams,
Save those seen in sweet summer dreams;
For sleeping in its bed of snow
Nor rock nor stone was ever known,
But only shining, shifting sands,
For ever sifted by unseen hands.

It curved, it bent like Indian bow,
And like an arrow darted through,
Yet utter'd not a sound nor breath,
Nor broke a ripple from the start;
It was as swift, as still as death,
Yet was so clear, so pure, so sweet,
It wound its way into your heart
As through the grasses at your feet.

Winnema's Face.

A FACE like hers is never seen
This side the gates of Paradise,
Save in some Indian-Summer scene,
And then none ever sees it twice—
Is seen but once, and seen no more,
Seen but to tempt the sceptic soul,
And show a sample of the whole
That Heaven has in store.

Loving Winnema.

YOU might have pluck'd beams from the moon,
Or torn the shadow from the pine
When on its dial track at noon,
But not have parted us an hour,
She was so wholly, truly mine.
And life was one unbroken dream
Of purest bliss, and calm delight,
A flow'ry-shored, untroubled stream
Of sun and song, of shade and bower,
A full-moon'd serenading night.

Sweet melodies were in the air,
And tame birds caroll'd everywhere.
I listen'd to the lisping grove

And cooing pink-eyed turtle-dove,
And, loving with the holiest love,
Believing with a grand belief,
That everything beneath the skies
Was beautiful and born to love;
That man had but to love, believe,
And earth would be a paradise
As beautiful as that above,
My goddess, Beauty, I adored,
Devoutly, fervid, her alone;
My Priestess, Love, unceasing pour'd
Pure incense on her altar-stone.

A-Faint.

My sinking soul fell just as far
As could a star loosed by a jar
From out the setting in the ring,
The purple, semi-circled ring
That seems to circle us at night.

Burning the Dead.

I laid my dead upon the pile,
And underneath the lisping oak
I watched the columns of dark smoke
Embrace her red lips, with a smile
Of frenzied fierceness. Then there came
A gleaming column of red flame,
That grew a grander monument
Above her nameless, noble mould,
Than ever bronze or marble lent
To king or conqueror of old.

It seized her in its hot embrace,
And leapt as if to reach the stars.
Then, looking up, I saw a face

So saintly and so sweetly fair,
So sad, so pitying, and so pure,
I nigh forgot the prison bars
And for one instant, one alone,
I felt I could forgive, endure.

I laid a circlet of white stone,
And left her ashes there alone.
But after many a white moon-wane
I sought that sacred ground again,
And saw the circle of white stone
With tall wild grasses overgrown.
I did expect, I know not why,
From out her sacred dust to find
Wild pinks and daisies blooming fair;
And when I did not find them there
I almost deemed her God unkind,
Less careful of her dust than I.

Lord Byron.

O COLD and cruel Nottingham!
In disappointment and in tears,
Sad, lost, and lonely, here I am
To question, "Is this Nottingham
Of which I dream'd for years and years?"
I seek in vain for name or sign
Of him, who made this mould a shrine,
A Mecca to the fair and fond
Beyond the seas, and still beyond.

In men whom men condemn as ill
I find so much of goodness still,
In men whom men pronounce divine
I find so much of sin and blot,
I hesitate to draw a line
Between the two, where God has not.

He stood—a solitary light
In stormy seas and settled night—
Then fell, but stirr'd the seas as far
As winds and waves and waters are.

To Robert Burns.

O Burns! where bid? where bide you now?
Where are you in this night's full noon,
Great master of the pen and plough?
Might you not on yon slanting beam
Of moonlight, kneeling to the Doon,
Descend once to this hallow'd stream?
Sure yon stars yield enough of light
For heaven to spare your face one night.

O sad, sweet singer of a Spring!
Yours was a chill uncheerful May,
And you knew no full days of June;
You ran too swiftly up the way,
And wearied soon, so over-soon!
You sang in weariness and woe;
You falter'd, and God heard you sing,
Then touch'd your hand and led you so,
You found life's hill-top low, so low,
You cross'd its summit long ere noon.
Thus, sooner than one would suppose,
Some weary feet will find repose.

The Moon on Winnema's Hair.

AND through the leaves the silver moon
Fell sifting down in silver bars
And play'd upon her raven hair,
And darted through like dimpled stars
That dance through all the night's sweet noon
To echoes of an unseen choir.

The Blame—a Prophecy.

I DID not blame you—do not blame.
The stormy elements of soul
That I did scorn to tone or tame,
Or bind down unto dull control
In full fierce youth, they all are yours,
With all their folly and their force.

God keep you pure, oh! very pure.
God give you grace to dare and do!
God give you courage to endure
The all He may demand of you,
Keep time-frosts from your raven hair,
And your young heart without a care.

I make no murmur nor complain;
Above me are the stars and blue
Alluring far to grand refrain;
Before, the beautiful and true,
To love or hate, to win or lose;
Lo! I will now arise and choose.

But should you sometime read a sign,
A name among the princely few,
In isles of song beyond the brine,
Then you will think a time, and you
Will turn and say, "He once was mine,
Was all my own; his smiles, his tears,
Were mine—were mine for years and years."

The Coffined Past.

LIFE knows no dead so beautiful
As is the white cold coffin'd past;
This I may love nor be betray'd:
The dead are faithful to the last.
I am not spouseless—I have wed
A memory—a life that's dead.

What Should Have Been.

Shadows that shroud the to-morrow
Glist from the life that's within,
Traces of pain and of sorrow,
And maybe a trace of sin,
Reachings for God in the darkness,
And for—what should have been.

A Poet of Nature.

In the shadows a-west of the sunset mountains,
Where old-time giants had dwelt and peopled,
And built up cities and castled battlements,
And rear'd up pillars that pierced the heavens,
A poet dwelt, of the book of Nature—
An ardent lover of the pure and beautiful,
Devoutest lover of the true and beautiful,
Profoundest lover of the grand and beautiful—
With a heart all impulse, intensest passion,
Who believed in love as in God Eternal—
A dream while the waken'd world went over,
An Indian summer of the sullen seasons;
And he sang wild songs like the winds in cedars,
Was tempest-toss'd as the pines, yet ever
As fix'd in truth as they in the mountains.

Woman's Strangeness.

Strangely wooing are the worlds above us,
Strangely beautiful is the Faith of Islam,
Strangely sweet are the songs of Solomon,
Strangely tender are the teachings of Jesus,
Strangely cold is the sun on the mountains,
Strangely mellow is the moon in old ruins,
Strangely pleasant are the stolen waters,

Strangely simple and unwooing is virtue,
Strangely lighted is the North night-region,
Strangely strong are the streams in the ocean,
Strangely true are the tales of the Orient,
Strangely winning is a dark-eyed widow,
Strangely wayward are the ways of lovers,
But, stranger than all are the ways of women.

Death.

DEATH is delightful. Death is dawn,
The waking from a weary night
Of fevers unto truth and light.
Fame is not much, love is not much,
Yet what else is there worth the touch
Of lifted hands with dagger drawn?
So surely life is little worth:
Therefore I say, look up; therefore
I say, One little star has more
Bright gold than all the earth of earth.

Recollection.

SOME things are sooner marred than made.
The moon was white, the stars a-chill—
A frost fell on a soul that night,
And lips were whiter, colder still.
A soul was black that erst was white.
And you forget the place—the night!
Forget that aught was done or said—
Say this has pass'd a long decade—
Say not a single tear was shed—
Say you forget these little things!
Is not your recollection loath?
Well, little bees have bitter stings,
And I remember for us both.

The Forest Maiden.

I LOVE
A forest maiden; she is mine;
And on Sierras' slopes of pine,
The vines below, the snows above,
A solitary lodge is set
Within a fringe of watered firs;
And there my wigwam fires burn,
Fed by a round, brown, patient hand,
That small brown faithful hand of hers
That never rests till my return.
The yellow smoke is rising yet;
Tiptoe, and see it where you stand
Lift like a column from the land.

There are no sea-gems in her hair;
No jewels fret her dimpled hands,
And half her bronzen limbs are bare:
But round brown arms have golden bands,
Broad, rich, and by her cunning hands
Cut from the yellow virgin ore,
And she does not desire more.
I wear the beaded wampum belt
That she has wove—the sable pelt
That she has fringed red threads around;
And in the morn, when men are not,
I wake the valley with the shot
That brings the brown deer to the ground;
And she beside the lodge at noon
Sings with the wind, while baby swings
In sea-shell cradle by the bough—
Sings low, so like the clover sings
With swarm of bees; I hear her now,
I see her sad face through the moon . . .
Such songs!—would earth had more of such!
She has not much to say, and she
Lifts never voice to question me
In aught I do . . . and that is much.

I love her for her patient trust,
And my love's forty fold return—
A value I have not to learn
As you—at least as many must.

She is not over tall or fair;
Her breasts are curtained by her hair,
And sometimes, through the silken fringe,
I see her bosom's wealth like wine,
Burst through in luscious ruddy tinge—
And all its wealth and worth are mine.
I know not that one drop of blood
Of prince or chief is in her veins:
I simply say that she is good,
And loves me with pure womanhood,
When that is said, why, what remains?

SONGS OF THE SUNLANDS.

BROUGHT out in 1873 by Longmans & Sons, London, and Roberts Brothers, Boston. Dedicated to the Rossettis. It consists of four long poems, and twenty-three short ones, the latter gathered under the titles "Olive Leaves" and "Fallen Leaves." The "Isles of the Amazons," the first and longest, was mostly composed in 1871, while drifting about on the Mexican and South Californian Pacific Coast, and appeared in the *Overland Monthly*. "In the Indian Summer" was composed at Cleveland, Ohio; "From Sea to Sea" and "Sierras Adios" in New York, the former being published in *Scribner's Monthly*. "Olive Leaves," which are sacred poems, were written in the Levant—some in the Holy Land and others about the Mediterranean, during 1872.

Well! who shall lay hand on my harp but me,
Or shall chide my song from the sounding trees?
The passionate sun and the resolute sea,
These were my masters, and only these.

I but sing for the love of song and the few
Who loved me first and shall love me last;
And the storm shall pass as the storms have pass'd,
For never were clouds but the sun came through.

The Rocky Mountains.

PRIMEVAL forests! virgin sod!
That Saxon hath not ravish'd yet!
Lo! peak on peak in column set,
In stepping stairs that reach to God!

Here we are free as sea or wind,
For here are set the snowy tents
In everlasting battlements,
Against the march of Saxon mind.

To the Cyprian Singer.

O CARPET-KNIGHT singer! shrewd merchant of song!
Get gold and be glad, buy, sell, and be strong!
Sweet Cyprian, I kiss you, I pay you, we part:
Go! you have my gold, but who has my heart?
Go, splendid-made singer, so finish'd, so fair,
Go sing you of heaven, with never a prayer,
Of hearts that are aching, with never a heart,
Of nature, all girded and bridled by art;
Go sing you of battles, with never a scar,
Of sunlight, with never a soul for the noon;
Move cold and alone like a broken, bright moon.
And shimmer and shine like a far, cold star.

In the Desert Wood.

UNTO God a prayer and to love a tear,
And I die, he said, in a desert here,
So deep that never a note is heard
But the listless song of that soulless bird.

The Knight Seeking Love.

I shall journey in search of the Incan Isles,
  Go far and away to traditional land,
Where Love is a queen in a crown of smiles,
  And battle has never imbrued a hand;

Where man has never despoiled or trod;
  Where woman's hand with a woman's heart
  Has fashion'd an Eden from man apart,
And she walks in her garden alone with God.

The Amazon Coast.

THE land was the tides; the shore was undone;
  It look'd as the lawless, unsatisfied seas
  Had thrust up an arm through the tangle of trees
And clutch'd at the citrons that grew in the sun;
  And clutch'd at the diamonds that hid in the sand,
  And laid heavy hand on the gold, and a hand
On the redolent fruits, on the ruby-like wine,
And the stones like the stars when the stars are divine.

The Song of the Silence.

O, HEAVENS, the eloquent song of the silence!
  Asleep lay the sun in the vines, on the sod,
And asleep in the sun lay the green-girdled islands,
  As rock'd to their rest in the cradle of God.

God's poet is silence! His song is unspoken,
  And yet so profound, so loud, and so far,
It fills you, it thrills you with measures unbroken,
  And as soft, and as fair, and as far as a star.

The shallow seas moan. From the first they have mutter'd
  And mourn'd, as a child, and have wept at their will . . .
The poems of God are too grand to be utter'd:
  The dreadful deep seas they are loudest when still.

The Queen of the Amazons.

With a face as brown as the boatmen's are,
Or the brave, brown hand of a harvester;
And girdled in gold, and crown'd in hair
In a storm of night, all studded with rare
Rich stones, that fretted the full of a noon,
The Queen on a prow stood splendid and tall,
As petulant waters would lift, and fall,
And beat, and bubble a watery rune.

The Love of the Trees.

The trees that lean'd in their love unto trees,
  That lock'd in their loves, and were so made strong,
Stronger than armies; ay, stronger than seas
  That rush from their caves in a storm of song.

Forsake the City.

Forsake the city. Follow me
To where the white caps of a sea
Of mountains break and break again,
  As blown in foam against a star—
As breaks the fury of a main—
  And there remains, as fix'd, as far.

Forsake the people. What are they
  That laugh, that live, that love by rule?
Forsake the Saxon. What are these
That shun the shadows of the trees:
The Druid-forests? . . . Go thy way,
We are not one. I will not please
  You:—fare you well, O wiser fool!

But you who love me;—Ye who love
  The shaggy forests, fierce delights
  Of sounding waterfalls, of heights
That hang like broken moons above,
With brows of pine that brush the sun,
Believe and follow. We are one;
The wild man shall to us be tame;
  The woods shall yield their mysteries;
The stars shall answer to a name,
  And be as birds above the trees.

Mountain Heights.

THE snow-topped towers crush the clouds
  And break the still abode of stars,
Like sudden ghosts in snowy shrouds,
  New broken through their earthly bars.

Isles of the Amazon.

O ISLES of a wave in an ocean of wood!
  O white waves lost in the wilds I love!
  Let the red stars rest on your breast from above,
And sing to the sun, for his love it is good.

He has made you his heirs, he has given you gold,
  And wrought for you garments of limitless green,
  With beautiful bars of the scarlet between,
And of silver seams fretting you fold on fold.

He has kiss'd and caress'd you, loved you true;
Yea, loved as a God loves, loved as I
Shall learn to love when the stars shall lie
Like blooms at my feet in a field of blue.

Amazon Beauties.

AND every color that the Master Sun
Has painted and hung in the halls of God,
Blush'd in the boughs or spread on the sod,
Pictured and woven and wound as one.

A bird in scarlet and gold, made mad
With sweet delights, through the branches slid,
And kiss'd the lake on a drowsy lid
Till the ripples ran and the face was glad.

The Tomb of Lovers.

THERE is many a love in the land, my love,
But never a love like this is:
Then kill me dead with your love, my love,
And cover me up with kisses.

So kill me dead and cover me deep
Where never a soul discovers;
Deep in your heart, to sleep, to sleep
In the darlingest tomb of lovers.

Alone by Thee.

O, PURE as a tear and as strong as a sea,
Yet tender to me as the touch of a dove,
I had rather sit sad and alone by thee,
Than to go and be glad, with a legion in love.

Let the Earth Rest.

It seems to me that Mother Earth
  Is weary from eternal toil
And bringing forth by fretted soil
  In all the agonies of birth.
Sit down! sit down! Lo, it were best
That we should rest, that she should rest.

I think we then shall all be glad,
At least I know we are not now;
Not one. And even Earth somehow
Seems growing old and over sad.
Then fold your hands, for it were best
That we should rest, that she should rest.

Love-lights.

I tell you that love is the bitterest sweet
  That ever laid hold on the heart of a man;
  A chain to the soul, and to cheer as a ban,
And a bane to the brain, and a snare to the feet.

Ay! who shall ascend on the hollow white wings
  Of love but to fall; to fall and to learn,
  Like a moth, and a man, that the lights lure to burn,
That the roses have thorns, and the honey-bee stings?

On and On.

On, on o'er the summit; and onward again,
And down like the sea-dove the billow enshrouds,
  And down like the swallow that dips to the sea,
  We dart and we dash and we quiver, and we
Are blowing to heaven white billows of clouds.

Love-sweets.

She is sweet as the breath of the Castile rose,
She is warm to the heart as a world of wine,
And as rich to behold as the rose that grows
With its red heart bent to the tide of the Rhine.

At Night in the Cars.

Lo! darkness bends down like a mother of grief
On the limitless plain, and the fall of her hair
It has mantled a world. The stars are in sheaf,
Yet onward we plunge like a beast in despair
Through the thick of the night; and the thundering cars!
They have crush'd and have broken the beautiful day;
Have crumbled it, scatter'd it far away,
And blown it above to a dust of stars.

The Pacific Reached.

We are hush'd with wonder and all apart
We stand in silence, till the heaving heart
Fills full of heaven, and then the knees
Go down in worship on the golden sands.
With faces seaward, and with folded hands
We gaze on the beautiful Balboa seas.

The Snow-Capped Sierras.

They stand white stairs of heaven,—stand a line
Of lifting, endless, and eternal white.
They look upon the far and flashing brine,
Upon the boundless plains, the broken height

Of Kamiakin's battlements. The flight
Of time is underneath their untopp'd towers.
They seem to push aside the moon at night,
To jostle and to loose the stars. The flowers
Of heaven fall about their brows in shining showers.

They stand a line of lifted snowy isles
High held above a toss'd and tumbled sea—
A sea of wood in wild unmeasured miles:
White pyramids of Faith where man is free;
White monuments of Hope, that yet shall be
The mounts of matchless and immortal song . . .
I look far down the hollow days: I see
The bearded prophets, simple-soul'd and strong,
That strike the sounding harp and thrill the heeding
throng.

Serene and satisfied! supreme! as lone
As God, they loom like God's archangels churl'd:
They look as cold as kings upon a throne:
The mantling wings of night are crush'd and curl'd
As feathers curl. The elements are hurl'd
From off their bosoms and are bidden go,
Like evil spirits, to an under-world.
They stretch from Cariboo to Mexico,
A line of battle-tents in everlasting snow.

On the Columbia.

An Indian summer-time it was, long past,
We lay on this Columbia, far below
The stormy water-falls, and God had cast
Us heaven's stillness. Dreamily and slow
We drifted as the light bark chose to go.
An Indian girl with ornaments of shell
Began to sing . . . The stars may hold such flow
Of hair, such eyes, but rarely earth. There fell
A sweet enchantment that possess'd me as a spell.

A Bison-King.

ONCE, morn by morn, when snowy mountains flam'd
With sudden shafts of light, that shot a flood
Into the vale like fiery arrows aim'd
At night from mighty battlements, there stood
Upon a cliff, high-limn'd against Mount Hood,
A matchless bull fresh forth from sable wold,
And standing so seem'd grander 'gainst the wood
Than wingèd bull, that stood with tips of gold
Beside the brazen gates of Nineveh of old.

A time he toss'd the dewy turf, and then
Stretch'd forth his wrinkled neck, and long and loud
He call'd above the far abodes of men
Until his breath became a curling cloud
And wreathed about his neck a misty shroud.

A Morn in Oregon.

A MORN in Oregon! The kindled camp
Upon the mountain brow that broke below
In steep and grassy stairway to the damp
And dewy valley, snapp'd and flamed aglow
With knots of pine. Above, the peaks of snow,
With under-belts of sable forests, rose
And flash'd in sudden sunlight. To and fro
And far below, in lines and winding rows,
The herders drove their bands and broke the deep repose.

I heard their shouts like sounding hunter's horn,
The lowing herds made echoes far away;
When lo! the clouds came driving in with morn
Toward the sea, as fleeing from the day.
The valleys fill'd with curly clouds. They lay
Below, a levell'd sea that reach'd and roll'd

And broke like breakers of a stormy bay
Against the grassy shingle fold on fold,
So like a splendid ocean, snowy white and cold.

Here lifts the land of clouds! The mantled forms,
Made white with everlasting snow, look down
Through mists of many cañons, and the storms
That stretch from Autumn time until they drown
The yellow hem of Spring. The cedars frown,
Dark-brow'd through banner'd clouds that stretch and stream
Above the sea from snowy mountain crown.
The heavens roll, and all things drift or seem
To drift about and drive like some majestic dream.

Sunshine after the Storm.

In waning Autumn time, when purpled skies
Begin to haze in indolence below
The snowy peaks, you see black forms arise
In rolling thunder banks above, and throw
Quick barricades about the gleaming snow.
The strife begins! The battling seasons stand
Broad breast to breast. A flash! Contentions grow
Terrific. Thunders crash, and lightnings brand
The battlements. The clouds possess the stormy land.

Then clouds blow by, the swans take loftier flight,
The yellow blooms burst out upon the hill,
The purple camas comes as in a night,
Tall spiked and dripping of the dews that fill
The misty valley . . . Sunbeams break and spill
Their glory till the vale is full of noon.
The roses belt the streams; no bird is still. . . .
The stars, as large as lilies, meet the moon
And sing of summer, born thus sudden full and soon.

To the Red Men, Sleeping.

My brave and unremember'd heroes, rest;
You fell in silence, silent lie and sleep.
Sleep on unsung, for this, I say, were best;
The world to-day has hardly time to weep;
The world to-day will hardly care to keep
In heart her plain and unpretending brave.
The desert winds, they whistle by and sweep
About you; brown'd and russet grasses wave
Along a thousand leagues that lie one common grave.

The proud and careless pass in palace car
Along the line you blazon'd white with bones;
Pass swift to people, and possess and mar
Your lands with monuments and letter'd stones
Unto themselves. Thank God! this waste disowns
Their touch. His everlasting hand has drawn
A shining line around you. Wealth bemoans
The waste your splendid grave employs. Sleep on,
No hand shall touch your dust this side of God and dawn.

The Red Men Still Free.

I have not been, shall not be understood;
I have not wit nor will to well explain,
But that which men call good I find not good.
The lands the savage held, shall hold again,
The gold the savage spurned in proud disdain
For centuries; go, take them all; build high
Your gilded temples; strive and strike and strain
And crowd and controvert and curse and lie
In church and state, in town and citadel, and—die.

And who shall grow the nobler from it all?
The mute and unsung savage loved as true,—
He felt, as grateful felt, God's blessings fall

About his lodge and tawny babes as you
In temples, Moslem, Christian monk, or Jew.
The sea, the great white, braided, bounding sea,
Is laughing in your face; the arching blue
Remains to God; the mountains still are free,
A refuge for the few remaining tribes and me.

Westminster Abbey.

THE Abbey broods beside the turbid Thames;
Her mother heart is fill'd with memories;
Her every niche is stored with storied names;
They move before me like a mist of seas.
I am confused, am made abash'd by these
Most kingly souls, grand, silent, and severe.
I am not equal, I should sore displease
The living . . . dead. I dare not enter; drear
And stain'd in storms of grander days all things appear.

The Indian Summer.

THE sunlight lay in gathered sheaves
Along the ground, the golden leaves
Possessed the land and lay in bars
Above the lifted lawn of green
Beneath the feet, or fell, as stars
Fall, slant-wise, shimmering and still
Upon the plain, upon the hill,
And heaving hill and plain between.

More than Fair.

. . . SHE was more than fair
And more than good, and matchless wise,
With all the lovelight in her eyes,
And all the midnight in her hair.

Look Starward.

LOOK starward; stand far and unearthly,
  Free-soul'd as a banner unfurl'd.
Be worthy, O brother, be worthy:
  For a God was the price of the world.

Hope.

WHAT song is well sung not of sorrow?
  What triumph well won without pain?
What virtue shall be and not borrow
  Bright lustre from many a stain?

A Wanderer.

A WANDERER of many lands
Was I, a weary Ishmaelite,
That knew the sign of lifted hands;
Had seen the Crescent-mosques, had seen
The Druid oaks of Aberdeen;
Then crossed the hilly seas, and saw
The sable pines of Mackinaw,
And lakes that lifted cold and white.

I saw the sweet Miami, saw
The swift Ohio bent and rolled
Between his gleaming walls of gold,
The Wabash banks of gray papaw,
The Mississippi's ash; at morn
Of autumn, when the oak is red,
Saw slanting pyramids of corn,
The level fields of spotted swine,
The crooked lanes of lowing kine,
And in the burning bushes saw
The face of God, with bended head.

Before a Poet's Shrine.

O MASTER, here I bow before a shrine;
Before the lordliest dust that ever yet
Moved animate in human form divine.
Lo! dust indeed to dust. The mould is set
Above thee and the ancient walls are wet,
And drip all day in dank and silent gloom,
As if the cold gray stones could not forget
Thy great estate shrunk to this sombre room,
But learn to weep perpetual tears above thy tomb.

The Indian-Summer Evening.

THE sun caught up his gathered sheaves;
A squirrel caught a nut, and ran;
A rabbit rustled in the leaves;
A whirling bat, black-winged and tan,
Blew swift between us; sullen night
Fell down upon us; mottled kine,
With lifted heads, went lowing down
The rocky ridge toward the town,
And all the woods grew dark as wine.

Bury Me Deep, my Beautiful Girl.

IF earth is an oyster, love is the pearl,
As pure as pure caresses;
Then loosen the gold of your hair, my girl,
And hide my pearl in your tresses.

So, coral to coral and pearl to pearl,
And a cloud of curls above me,
O bury me deep, my beautiful girl,
And then confess you love me.

A Coming Storm.

A SINKING sun, a sky of red,
In bars and banners overhead,
And blown apart like curtains drawn;
Afar a-sea a blowing sail
That shall go down before the dawn;
And they are passion-toss'd and pale—
The two that stand and look alone
And silent, as two shafts of stone
Set head and foot above the dead.

My Song Sung.

WITH buckler and sword into battle
I moved, I was matchless and strong;
I stood in the rush and the rattle
Of shot, and the spirit of song
Was upon me; and youthful and splendid
My armor flashed far in the sun
As I sang of my land. It is ended,
And all has been done, and undone.

Adieu.

WELL, we have threaded through and through
The gloaming forests. Fairy Isles,
Afloat in sun and summer smiles,
As fallen stars in fields of blue.
Some futile wars with subtile love
That mortal never vanquished yet,
Some symphonies by angels set
In wave below, in bough above,
Were yours and mine; but here adieu.

My Graves.

I DESCEND with my dead in the trenches,
To-night I bend down on the plain
In the dark, and a memory wrenches
The soul; I turn up to the rain
The cold and beautiful faces,
Ay, faces forbidden for years,
Turn'd up to my face with the traces
Of blood to the white rain of tears.

Count backward the years on your fingers,
While forward rides yonder white moon,
Till the soul turns aside, and it lingers
By a grave that was born of a June;
By a grave of a soul, where the grasses
Are tangled as witch-woven hair;
Where foot-prints are not, and where passes
Not anything known anywhere.

By a grave without tombstone or token,
At a tomb where not fern leaf or fir,
Root or branch, was once bended or broken,
To bestow there the body of her;
For it lives, and the soul perish'd only,
And alone in that land, with these hands,
Did I lay the dead soul, and all lonely
Does it lie to this day in the sands.

Patience.

IT is well, may be so, to bear losses,
And to bend and bow down to the rod;
If the scarlet red bars and the crosses
Be but rounds up the ladder to God.

Charity.

Her hands were clasped downward and doubled,
Her head was held down and depress'd;
Her bosom, like white billows troubled,
Fell fitful and rose in unrest;

Her robes were all dust, and disorder'd
Her glory of hair, and her brow,
Her face, that had lifted and lorded,
Fell pallid and passionless now.

She heard not accusers that brought her
In mockery hurried to Him,
Nor heeded, nor said, nor besought her
With eyes lifted doubtful and dim.

All crush'd and stone-cast in behavior,
She stood as a marble would stand;
Then the Saviour bent down, and the Saviour
In silence wrote on in the sand.

What wrote He? How fondly one lingers
And questions, what holy command
Fell down from the beautiful fingers
Of Jesus, like gems in the sand.

O better the Scian uncherish'd
Had died ere a note or device
Of battle was fashion'd, than perish'd
This only line written by Christ.

He arose and he look'd on the daughter
Of Eve, like a delicate flower,
And he heard the revilers that brought her—
Men stormy, and strong as a tower;

And he said, "She has sinn'd; let the blameless
Come forward and cast the first stone!"

But they, they fled shamed and yet shameless;
And she, she stood white and alone.

Who now shall accuse and arraign us?
What man shall condemn and disown?
Since Christ has said only the stainless
Shall cast at his fellows a stone.

For what man can bare us his bosom,
And touch with his forefinger there,
And say, 'Tis as snow, as a blossom?
Beware of the stainless, beware!

O woman, born first to believe us;
Yea, also born first to forget;
Born first to betray and deceive us,
Yet first to repent and regret!

O first then in all that is human,
Lo! first where the Nazarene trod,
O woman! O beautiful woman!
Be then first in the kingdom of God!

The Amazon.

It was dark and dreadful! Wide like an ocean,
Much like a river but more like a sea,
Save that there was naught of the turbulent motion
Of tides, or of winds blown back, or a-lee.

Yea, strangely strong was the wave and slow,
And half-way hid in the dark deep tide,
Great turtles they paddled them to and fro,
And away to the Isles and the opposite side.

The nude black boar through abundant grass
Stole down to the water and buried his nose,
And crush'd white teeth till the bubbles rose
As white and as bright as the globes of glass.

Yea, steadily moved it, mile upon mile,
  Above and below and as still as the air;
  The bank made slippery here and there
By the slushing slide of the crocodile.

The Lost Knight.

"I SHALL die," he said, "by the solemn deep river,
  By the king of the rivers, and the mother of seas,
So far, and so far from my Guadalquiver,
  Near, and so near to the dreaded Andes.

"Let me sing one song by the grand old river,
  And die;" and he reach'd and he brake him a reed
From the rim of the river, where they lift and quiver,
  And he trimm'd it and notch'd it with all his speed.

With his treacherous blade, in the sweep of the trees,
  As he stood with his head bent low on his breast,
And the vines in his hair and the wave to his knees,
  And bow'd like to one who would die to rest.

"I shall fold my hands, for this is the river
  Of death," he said, "and the sea-green Isle
Is an Eden set by the gracious Giver
  Wherein to rest." He listened the while,

Then lifted his head, then lifted a hand
  Arch'd over his brow, and he lean'd and listen'd—
'Twas only a bird on a border of sand,—
  The dark stream eddy'd and gleam'd and glisten'd

Stately and still as the march of a moon,
  And the martial notes from the Isle were gone,—
  Gone as a dream dies out with the dawn,
And gone as far as the night from the noon.

Music in the Forest.

THE quick leaves quiver'd, and the sunlight danced;
As the boy sang sweet, and the birds said, "Sweet;"
And the tiger crept close, and lay low at his feet,
And he sheath'd his claws in the sun, entranced.

The serpent that hung from the sycamore bough,
And sway'd his head in a crescent above,
Had folded his neck to the white limb now,
And fondled it close like a great black love.

The Fainting Knight.

THEN gently as touch of the truest of woman,
They lifted him up from the earth as he fell,
And into the boat, with a half-hidden swell
Of the heart that was holy and tenderly human.

They spoke low-voiced as a vesper prayer;
They pillowed his head as only the hand
Of woman can pillow, and push'd from the land,
And the Queen she sat threading the gold of his hair.

Then away with the wave, and away to the Isles,
In a song of the oars of the crescented fleet,
That timed together in musical wiles
In bubbles of melodies swift and sweet.

The Storm Shall Pass.

'Mid white Sierras, that slope to the sea,
Lie turbulent lands. Go dwell in the skies,
And the thundering tongues of Yosemité
Shall persuade you to silence, and you shall be wise.

Yea, men may deride, and the thing it is well;
  Turn well and aside from the one wild note
  To the song of the bird with the tame, sweet throat;
But the sea sings on in his cave and shell.

Let the white moons ride, let the red stars fall,
  O great, sweet sea! O fearful and sweet!
  Thy songs they repeat, and repeat, and repeat:
And these, I say, shall survive us all.

I but sing for the love of song and the few
  Who loved me first and shall love me last;
  And the storm shall pass as the storms have pass'd,
For never were clouds but the sun came through.

The Origin of Man.

In the days when my mother, the Earth, was young,
  And you all were not, nor the likeness of you,
She walk'd in her maidenly prime among
  The moonlit stars in the boundless blue.

Then the great sun lifted his shining shield,
  And he flash'd his sword as the soldiers do,
And he moved like a king full over the field,
  And he look'd, and he loved her brave and true.

And looking afar from the ultimate rim
  As he lay at rest in a reach of light,
  He beheld her walking alone at night,
Where the buttercup stars in their beauty swim.

So he rose up flush'd in his love, and he ran,
  And he reach'd his arms, and around her waist
He wound them strong like a love-struck man,
  And he kiss'd and embraced her, brave and chaste.

So he nursed his love like a babe at its birth,
And he warm'd in his love as the long years ran,
Then embraced her again, and sweet mother Earth
Was a mother indeed, and her child was man.

The sun is the sire, the mother is earth!
What more do you know? what more do I need?
The one he begot, and the one gave birth,
And I love them both, and let laugh at your creed.

Gold.

I KNOW upon this earth a spot
Where clinking coins, that clink as chains
Upon the souls of men, are not;
Nor man is measured for his gains
Of gold that stream with crimson stains.

The rivers run unmaster'd yet,
Unmeasured sweep their sable bredes:
The pampas unpossess'd is set
With stormy banners of her steeds,
That rival man in martial deeds.

O men that fret as frets the main!
You irk one with your eager gaze
Down in the earth for fat increase—
Eternal talks of gold and gain,
Your shallow wit, your shallow ways . .
And breaks my soul across the shoal
As breakers break on shallow seas.

The Lake.

AND strangely still, and more strangely sweet,
Was the lake that lay in its cradle of fern,
As still as a moon with her horns that turn
In the night, like lamps to some delicate feet.

On the Isles.

AND here the carpets of Nature were spread,
Made pink with blossoms and fragrant bloom;
Her soft couch, canopied overhead,
Allured to sleep with the deep perfume.

The sarsaparilla had woven its thread
So through and through, like the threads of gold;
'Twas stronger than thongs in its thousandfold,
And on every hand and up overhead

Ran thick as threads on the rim of a reel,
Through red leaf and dead leaf, bough and vine,
The green and the gray leaf, coarse and fine,
And the cactus tinted with cochineal.

Watching the Bathers.

THE great trees shadow'd the bow-tipp'd tide,
And nodded their plumes from the opposite side,
As if to whisper, Take care! take care!
But the meddlesome sunshine here and there,

Kept pointing a finger right under the trees,—
Kept shifting the branches and wagging a hand
At the round brown limbs on the border of sand,
And seem'd to whisper, Ho! what are these?

The gold-barr'd butterflies to and fro
And over the waterside wander'd and wove
As heedless and idle as clouds that rove
And drift by the peaks of perpetual snow.

A monkey swung out from a bough in the skies,
White whisker'd and ancient, and wisest of all
Of his populous race, and he heard them call
And he watch'd them long, with his head sidewise,

From under his brows of amber and brown,
All patient and silent and never once stirr'd ;
Then he shook his head and he hasten'd him down
To his army below and said never a word.

The New Land of Song.

WHEN spires shall shine on the Amazon's shore,
From temples of God, and time shall have roll'd
Like a scroll from the border the limitless wold;
When the tiger is tamed, and the mono no more

Swings over the waters to chatter and call
To the crocodile sleeping in rushes and fern;
When cities shall gleam, and their battlements burn
In the sunsets of gold, where the cocoa-nuts fall;

'Twill be something to lean from the stars and to know
That the engine, red-mouthing with turbulent tongue,
The white ships that come, and the cargoes that go,
We invoked them of old when the nations were young:

'Twill be something to know that we named them of old,—
That we said to the nations, Lo! here is the fleece
That allures to the rest, and the perfectest peace,
With its foldings of sunlight shed mellow like gold:

That we were the Carsons in kingdoms untrod,
And follow'd the trail through the rustle of leaves,
And stood by the wave where solitude weaves
Her garments of mosses, and lonely as God:

That we did make venture when singers were young,
Inviting from Europe, from long-trodden lands
That are easy of journeys, and holy from hands
Laid upon by the Masters when giants had tongue:

The prophet should lead us,—and lifting a hand
To the world on the way, like a white guiding star,
Point out and allure to the fair and unknown,
And the far, and the hidden delights of a land.

Behold my Sierras! there singers shall throng;
The Andes shall break through the wings of the night
As the fierce condor breaks through the clouds in his flight;
And I here plant the Cross and possess them with song.

Across the Continent.

WE glide through golden seas of grain;
We shoot, a shining comet, through
The mountain range against the blue
And then below the walls of snow,
We blow the desert dust amain;
We brush the gay madrona tree,
We greet the orange groves below,—
We rest beneath the oaks; and we
Have cleft a continent in twain.

The Lakes and the West.

O SEAS in a land! O lakes of mine!
By the love I bear and the songs I bring
Be glad with me! lift your waves and sing
A song in the reeds that surround your isles!
A song of joy for this sun that smiles,
For this land I love and this age and sign;
For the peace that is and the perils pass'd;
For the hope that is and the rest at last!

O heart of the world's heart! West! my West!
Look up! look out! There are fields of kine,

There are clover-fields that are red as wine ;
And a world of kine in the fields take rest,
And ruminate in the shade of trees
That are white with blossoms or brown with bees.

There are emerald seas of corn and cane;
There are cotton-fields like a foamy main,
To the far-off South where the sun was born,
Where the fair have birth and the loves knew morn.
There are isles of oak and a harvest plain,
Where brown men bend to the bending grain ;
There are temples of God and towns new-born,
And beautiful homes of beautiful brides ;
And the hearts of oak and the hands of horn
Have fashion'd them all and a world besides.

The Sweetest.

SWEETER than swans are a maiden's graces !
  Sweeter than fruits are the kisses of morn !
  Sweeter than babes is a love new-born,
But sweeter than all are a love's embraces.

Down into the Dust.

Is it worth while that we jostle a brother
  Bearing his load on the rough road of life ?
Is it worth while that we jeer at each other
  In blackness of heart?—that we war to the knife ?
  God pity us all in our pitiful strife.

God pity us all as we jostle each other;
  God pardon us all for the triumphs we feel
When a fellow goes down 'neath his load on the heather,
  Pierced to the heart : words are keener than steel,
  And mightier far for woe or for weal.

Is it worth while that we battle to humble
  Some poor fellow-soldier down into the dust?
God pity us all! Time eftsoon will tumble
  All of us together like leaves in a gust,
  Humbled indeed down into the dust.

Palm Leaves.

THATCH of palm and a patch of clover,
  Breath of balm in a field of brown,
The clouds blew up and the birds flew over,
  And I look'd upward; but who look'd down?

Who was true in the test that tried us?
  Who was it mock'd? Who now may mourn
The loss of a love that a cross denied us,
  With folded hands and a heart forlorn?

God forgive when the fair forget us.
  The worth of a smile, the weight of a tear,
Why, who can measure? The fates beset us.
  We laugh a moment; we mourn a year.

At Bethlehem.

WITH incense and myrrh and sweet spices,
  Frankincense and sacredest oil
In ivory, chased with devices
  Cut quaint and in serpentine coil,
Heads bared, and held down to the bosom;
  Brows massive with wisdom and bronzed;
Beards white as the white May in blossom,
  And borne to the breast and beyond,—
Came the Wise of the East, bending lowly
  On staffs, with their garments girt round

With girdles of hair, to the Holy
  Child Christ, in their sandals. The sound
Of song and thanksgiving ascended—
  Deep night! Yet some shepherds afar
Heard a wail with the worshipping blended,
  And they then knew the sign of the star.

Unrest.

When we most need rest, and the perfect sleep,
Some hand will reach from the dark, and keep
The curtains drawn and the pillows toss'd
Like a tide of foam; and one will say
At night,—O Heaven, that it were day!
And one by night through the misty tears
Will say,—O Heaven, the days are years,
And I would to Heaven that the waves were cross'd.

In Yosemite Valley.

Sound! sound! sound!
O colossal walls, as crown'd
In one eternal thunder!
Sound! sound! sound!
O ye oceans overhead,
While we walk, subdued in wonder,
In the ferns and grasses, unde
And beside the swift Merced!

Sweep! sweep! sweep!
O ye heaven-born and deep,
In one dread, unbroken chorus!
We may wonder or may weep,—
We may wait on God before us;
We may shout or lift a hand,—
We may bow down and deplore us,
But may never understand.

Beat! beat! beat!
We advance, but would retreat
From this restless, broken breast
Of the earth in a convulsion.
We would rest, but dare not rest,
For the angel of expulsion
From this Paradise below
Waves us onward and . . . we go.

Faith.

THERE were whimsical turns of the waters,
There were rhythmical talks of the sea,—
There were gather'd the darkest-eyed daughters
Of men, by the dark Galilee.

A blowing full sail, and a parting
From multitudes, living in him,
A trembling of lips, and tears starting
From eyes that look'd downward and dim.

A mantle of night and a marching
Of storms, and a sounding of seas,
Of furrows of foam and of arching
Black billows; a bending of knees;
The rising of Christ—an entreating—
Hands reach'd to the seas as he saith,
"Have Faith!" And lo! still are repeating
All seas, "Have Faith! Have Faith! Have Faith!"

Beyond Jordan.

AND they came to him, mothers of Judah,
Dark-eyed and in splendor of hair,
Bearing down over shoulders of beauty,
And bosoms half hidden, half bare;

And they brought him their babes and besought him
  Half kneeling, with suppliant air,
To bless the brown cherubs they brought him,
  With holy hands laid in their hair.

Then reaching his hands he said, lowly,
  "Of such is my Kingdom;" and then
Took the brown little babes in the holy
  White hands of the Saviour of men;

Held them close to his heart and caress'd them,
  Put his face down to theirs as in prayer,
Put their hands to his neck, and so bless'd them
  With baby hands hid in his hair.

The Last Supper.

WHAT song sang the twelve with the Saviour
  When finish'd the sacrament wine?
Were they bow'd and subdued in behavior,
  Or bold as made bold with a sign?

What sang they? What sweet song of Zion
  With Christ in their midst like a crown?
While here sat Saint Peter, the lion;
  And there like a lamb, with head down,

Sat Saint John, with his silken and raven
  Rich hair on his shoulders, and eyes
Lifting up to the faces unshaven
  Like a sensitive child's in surprise.

Was the song as strong fishermen swinging
  Their nets full of hope to the sea?
Or low, like the ripple-wave, singing
  Sea-songs on their loved Galilee?

Were they sad with foreshadow of sorrows,
  Like the birds that sing low when the breeze

Is tip-toe with a tale of to-morrows,—
Of earthquakes and sinking of seas?

Ah! soft was their song as the waves are
That fall in low musical moans;
And sad I should say as the winds are
That blow by the white gravestones.

The Nazarene.

THE years may lay hand on fair heaven;
May place and displace the red stars;
May stain them, as blood-stains are driven
At sunset in beautiful bars;

May shroud them in black till they fret us
As clouds with their showers of tears;
May grind us to dust and forget us,
May the years, O, the pitiless years!

The precepts of Christ are beyond them;
The truths by the Nazarene taught,
With the tramp of the ages upon them,
They endure as though ages were nought.

A Resting-Place.

I KNOW a grassy slope above the sea,
The utmost limit of the westmost land.
In savage, gnarl'd and antique majesty
The great trees belt about the place, and stand
In guard, with mailèd limb and lifted head
Against the cold approaching civic pride.
The foamy brooklets seaward leap; the bland
Still air is fresh with touch of wood and tide,
And peace, eternal peace, possesses wild and wide.

Here I return, here I abide and rest;
Some flocks and herds shall feed along the stream;
Some corn and climbing vines shall make us blest
With bread and luscious fruit . . . The sunny dream
Of savage men in moccasins, that seem
To come and go in silence, girt in shell,
Before a sun-clad cabin-door, I deem
The harbinger of peace. Hope weaves her spell
Again about the wearied heart, and all is well.

Here I shall sit in sunlit life's decline
Beneath my vine and sombre verdant tree.
Some tawny maids in other tongues than mine
Shall minister. Some memories shall be
Before me. I shall sit and I shall see,
That last vast day that dawn shall re-inspire,
The sun fall down upon the farther sea,
Fall wearied down to rest, and so retire,
A splendid sinking isle of far-off fading fire.

Remembrance.*

O BOY at peace upon the Delaware!
O brother mine, that fell in battle front
Of life, so braver, nobler far than I,
The wanderer who vexed all gentleness,
Receive this song; I have but this to give.
I may not rear the rich man's ghostly stone;
But you, through all my follies loving still
And trusting me . . . nay, I shall not forget.

A failing hand in mine, and fading eyes
That look'd in mine as from another land,
You said: "Some gentler things; a song for Peace.
'Mid all your songs for men one song for God."
And then the dark-brow'd mother, Death, bent down
Her face to yours, and you were born to Him.

* A prelude to "Olive Leaves." The brother alluded to was, perhaps, the nearest of all friends to Mr. Miller's heart, because he understood and believed in him. He died at Easton, Penn., in 1871.

UNWRITTEN HISTORY;

OR,

LIFE AMONGST THE MODOCS.

THIS book was begun in California—upon the author's return after an absence of twelve years—as an autobiography, but was mostly composed in London. The opening chapters, which abound in descriptions of the Mount Shasta regions, were written amid their sublime scenery, and by the council fires of the Shasta and Modoc tribes of Indians. When asked how much of truth there was in the narrative, the reply of the author was, "More than poetry." It is, in fact, his life with embellishments. Published first by Richard Bentley & Sons, London, and afterward by the American Publishing Co., Hartford, Conn., in 1873.

Mistaken and misunderstood,
My hot magnetic heart sought round
And craved of all the souls I knew
But one responsive throb or touch,
Or thrill that flashes through and through.
Deem you that I demanded much? . . .
Not one congenial soul was found.

Shasta Unrivalled.

LONELY as God, and white as a winter moon, Mount Shasta starts up sudden and solitary from the heart of the great black forests of Northern California. You would hardly call Mount Shasta a part of the Sierras; you would say rather that it is the great white tower of some ancient and eternal wall, with here and there the white walls overthrown.

It has no rival! There is not even a snow-crowned subject in sight of its dominion. A shining pyramid in mail of everlasting frosts and ice, the sailor sometimes, in a day of singular clearness, catches glimpses of it from the sea a hundred miles away to the west; and it may be seen from the dome of the capital three hundred miles distant. The immigrant coming from the east beholds the snowy, solitary pillar from afar out on the arid sage-brush plains, and lifts his hands in silence as in answer to a sign.

Trojan Miners.

THESE are mining camps. Men are there, down in these dreadful cañons, out of sight of the sun, swallowed up, buried in the impenetrable gloom of the forests, toiling for gold. Each one of these camps is a world in itself. History, romance, tragedy, poetry in every one of them. They are connected together, and reach the outer world only by a narrow little pack trail, stretching through the timber, stringing round the mountains, barely wide enough to admit of footmen and little Mexican mules with their apparajos, to pass in single file. We will descend into one of these camps by-and-by. I dwelt there a year, many and many a year ago. I shall picture that camp as it was, and describe events as they happened. Giants were there, great men were there. They were very strong, energetic and resolute, and hence were neither gentle or sympathetic. They were honorable, noble, brave and generous, and yet they would have dragged a Trojan around the wall by the heels and thought nothing of it. Coming suddenly into the country with prejudices against and apprehensions of the Indians, of whom they knew nothing save through novels, they of course were in no mood to study their nature. Besides, they knew that they were in a way, trespassers if not invaders, that the Government had never treated for the land or offered any terms whatever to the Indians, and like most men who feel that they are somehow in the wrong, do not care to get on terms with their antagonists. They would have named the Indian a Trojan, and dragged him around, not only by the heels but by the scalp, rather than taken time or trouble, as a rule, to get in the right of the matter.

I say that the greatest, the grandest body of men that have ever been gathered together since the siege of Troy, was once here on the Pacific. I grant that they were rough enough sometimes. I admit that they took a peculiar delight in periodical six-shooter war-dances, these wild-bearded, hairy-breasted men, and that they did a great deal of promiscuous killing among each other, but then they did it in such a manly sort of way!

A Beaver Hat.

THESE men of the mountains always have despised and perhaps always will despise a beaver hat. Why? Here is food for reflection. Here is a healthy, well-seated antipathy to an innocent article of dress, without any discovered reason. Let the profound look into this.

As for myself, I have looked into this thing, but am not satisfied. The only reason I can give for this enmity to the "tile" in the mountains of California, is not that the miners hold that there is anything wrong in the act or fact of a man wearing a beaver, but because it invests the man with a dignity—an artificial dignity, it is true, but none the less a dignity—too far above that of a man who wears a slouch or felt. The beaver hat is the minority, the slouch hat is the majority; and, like all great majorities, is a mob—a cruel, heartless, arrogant, insolent mob, ignorant and presumptive. The beaver hat is a missionary among cannibals in the California mines. And the saddest part of it all is, that there is no hope of reform. Tracts on this subject would be useless. Fancy a beaver hat in a dripping tunnel, or by the splashing flume or dumping derrick!

Born of a low element in our nature is this antagonism to the beaver hat; cruel as it is curious, selfish, but natural.

The Englishman knows well the power and dignity of a beaver hat. Go into the streets of London and look about you. Surely some power has issued an order not much unlike that of the famous one-armed sailor—"England expects every man to wear a beaver hat."

Opposition to a Coin Currency.

For my own part, I would banish gold and silver, as a commercial medium, from the face of the earth. I would abolish the use of gold and silver altogether, have paper currency, and but one currency in all the world. I propose to take all the strong men now in the mines down from the mountains, and build ships and cities by the sea, and make a permanent commonwealth.

These thousands of men can, at best, in a year's time, only take out a few millions of gold. A ship goes to sea and sinks with all these millions, and thus all that labor is lost to the world forever. Had these millions been in paper, only a few hours' labor would have been lost. There are two hundred thousand men, the best and bravest men in the world, wasting the best years of their lives getting out this gold. They are turning over the mountains, destroying the forests, filling up the rivers. They make the land unfit even for savages. Take them down from the mountains, throw one-half of their strength and energy against the wild, rich sea-border of the Pacific, and we would have, instead of these broken mountains, muddied rivers, and ruined forests, such an Eden as has not been seen by man since the days of Adam.

An Explosion.

A DULL crash, a dreadful sound that has no name, and cannot be described, started me to my feet. Bark and poles and pieces of wood came raining on our roof; then there was not a sound, not even a whisper.

The poor Indian, so accustomed to arrange and prepare their arms and such things by the camp fire, had forgotten my caution perhaps, for somehow the powder had, while the Indians were unpacking and arranging it in the lodge, ignited, and they, and all the fruits of our hard and reckless enterprise, were blown to nothing.

The Indians of the camp, and the three surviving companions of my venture, were overcome. Their old superstition returned. They sat down with their backs to the dead bodies, hid their faces, and waited till the medicine-man came from the camp on the lake below.

About midnight the women began to wail for the dead from the hills. What a wail, and what a night!

There is no sound so sad, so heartbroken and pitiful, as this long and sorrowful lamentation. Sometimes it is almost savage, it is loud, fierce, and vehement; your heart sinks, you sympathize, and you think of your own dead, and you lament with them the common lot of man. Then your soul widens out, and you begin to go down with them to the shore of the dark water, to stand there, to be with them and of them, there in the great mysterious shadow of death, to feel how much we are all alike, and how little difference there is in the destinies, the sorrows, and the sympathies of the children of men.

The Faithful Heroine.

SHE came about midnight, the true and faithful little savage, the heroine, the red star of my dreadful life, crouching on the roof, and laid hold of the bars one by one, and bent them till I could pass my head and shoulders. Then she drew me through, almost carried me in her arms, and in another moment we touched the steep but solid earth.

She hurried me up the hill-side to the edge of a thicket of chaparral. I could go no further. I fell upon my knees and clasped my hands. I bent down my face and kissed and kissed the earth as you would kiss a sister you had not seen for years. I arose and clasped the bushes in my arms, and stripped the fragrant myrtle-leaves by handfuls. I kissed my hands to the moon, the stars, and began to shout and leap like a child. She laid her hand on my mouth, and almost angrily seized me by the arm. I turned and I kissed her, or rather only the presence and touch of her. I lifted her fingers to my lips, her robe, her hair, as she led me over the hill, around and down to a trail. There, in answer to the night-bird call, an Indian, a brave, reckless fellow, who had been with me in many a bold adventure, led three horses from a thicket.

A California Moon.

WHAT a glorious moon! Only such a moon as California can afford. A long white cloud of swans stretched overhead, croaking dolefully enough; the sea of evergreen pines that rolled about the bluff and belted the base of Shasta was sable as a pall, but the snowy summit in the splendors of the moon, flashed like a pyramid of silver! All these mountains, all these mighty forests, were to me as a school-boy's play-ground, the playmates gone, the master dead!

In the Shadow of the Pines.

TO-DAY, when the sun was low, we sat down in the shadow of the pines on a mossy trunk, a little way out from the door. The sun threw lances against the shining mail of Shasta, and they glanced aside and fell, quivering, at our feet, on the quills and dropping acorns. A dreamy sound of waters came up through the tops of the alder and madroño trees below us.

At Peace.

THE world, no doubt, went on in its strong, old way, afar off, but we did not hear it. The sailing of ships, the conventions of men, the praise of men, and the abuse of men; the gathering together of the fair in silks, and laces, and diamonds under the lights; the success or defeat of this measure or of that man; profit and loss; the rise and fall of stocks: what were they all to us?

Peace! After many a year of battle with the world, we had retreated, thankful for a place of retreat, and found rest—peace. Now and then an acorn dropped;

now and then an early leaf fell down; and once I heard the whistle of an antlered deer getting his herd together to lead them down the mountain; but that was all that broke the perfect stillness. A chipmunk dusted across the burrs, mounted the further end of the mossy trunk, lifted on his hind legs, and looked all around; then, finding no hand against him, let himself down, ran past my elbow on to the ground again, and gathered in his paws, then into his mouth, an acorn at our feet. Peace! Peace! Who, my little brown neighbor in the striped jacket, who would have allowed you to take that, even that acorn, in peace, down in the busy, battling world? But we are above it. The storms of the social sea may blow, the surf may break against the rocky base of this retreat, may even sweep a little way into the sable fringe of firs, but it shall never reach us here.

Mount Shasta.

COLUMN upon column of storm-stained tamarack, strong-tossing pines, and warlike-looking firs have rallied here. They stand with their backs against this mountain, frowning down, dark-browed, and confronting the face of the Saxon. They defy the advance of civilization into their ranks. What if these dark and splendid columns, a hundred miles in depth, should be the last to go down in America! What if this should be the old guard gathered here, marshalled around their emperor in plumes and armor, that may die but not surrender! Ascend this mountain, stand against the snow above the upper belt of pines, and take a glance below. Toward the sea nothing but the black and unbroken forest. Mountains, it is true, dip and divide and break the monotony as the waves break up the sea; yet it is still the sea, still the unbroken forest, black and magnificent. To the south the landscape sinks and declines gradually, but still

maintains its column of dark-plumed grenadiers, till the Sacramento Valley is reached, nearly a hundred miles away. Silver rivers run here, the sweetest in the world. They wind and wind among the rocks and mossy roots, with California lilies, and the yew with scarlet berries dipping in the water, and trout idling in the eddies and cool places by the basketful. On the east, the forest still keeps up unbroken rank till the Pit River valley is reached; and even there it surrounds the valley, and locks it up tight in its black embrace.

Camp Life in the Wood.

THE wood seemed very, very beautiful. The air was so rich, so soft and pure in the Indian Summer, that it almost seemed that you could feed upon it. The antlered deer, fat and tame almost as if fed in parks, stalked by, and game of all kinds filled the woods in herds. We hunted, rode, fished and rested beside the rivers. What a fragrance from the long and bent fir boughs; what a healthy breath of pine! All the long sweet moonlight nights the magnificent forest, warm and mellow-like from sunshine gone away, gave out odors like burnt offerings from censers swinging in some mighty cathedral.

Mount Hood.

HOOD is rugged, kingly, majestic, immortal! But he is only the head and front of a well-raised family. He is not alone in his splendor. Your admiration is divided and weakened. Beyond the Columbia, St. Helen's flashes in the sun in summer or is folded in clouds from the sea in winter. On either hand Jefferson and Washington divide the attention; then farther away, fair as a stud of fallen stars, the white Three Sisters are grouped together about the fountain springs of the Willamette river; all in a line—all in one range of mountains; as it were, mighty milestones along the way of clouds!—marble pillars pointing the road to God!

An Indian Likeness.

FOR want of a truer comparison let us liken him to a jealous woman—a whole-souled, uncultured woman, strong in her passions and her love. A sort of Parisian woman, now made desperate by a long siege and an endless war.

Shasta and Hood.

MOUNT SHASTA has all the sublimity, all the strength, majesty and magnificence of Hood; yet is so alone, unsupported and solitary, that you go down before him utterly with an undivided adoration—a sympathy for his loneliness and a devotion for his valor—an admiration that shall pass unchallenged.

First Glimpse of Shasta.

MOUNT SHASTA was before me. For the first time I now looked upon the mountain in whose shadows so many tragedies were to be enacted; the most comely and perfect snow-peak in America. Nearly a hundred miles away, it seemed in the pure, clear atmosphere of the mountains to be almost at hand. Above the woods, above the clouds, almost above the snow, it looked like the first approach of land to another world. Away across a gray sea of clouds that arose from the Klamat and Shasta rivers, the mountain stood, a solitary island; white and flashing like a pyramid of silver! Solemn, majestic and sublime! Lonely and cold and white. A cloud or two about his brow, sometimes resting there, then wreathed and coiled about, then blown like banners streaming in the wind.

The Freemasonry of Mountain Scenery.

NEVER, until on some day of storms in the lower world you have ascended one mountain, looked out above the clouds, and seen the white snowy pyramids piercing here and there the rolling nebulous sea, can you hope to learn the freemasonry of mountain scenery in its grandest, highest and most supreme degree. Lightning and storms and thunder underneath you; calm and peace and perfect beauty about you! Typical and suggestive.

A Glimpse of the Sierras.

THIS cañon was as black as Erebus down there—a sea of sombre firs; and down, down as if the earth were cracked and cleft almost in two. Here and there lay little nests of clouds below us, tangled in the tree-tops, no wind to drive them, nothing to fret and disturb. They lay above the dusks of the forest as if asleep. Over across the cañon stood another mountain, not so fierce as this, but black with forest, and cut and broken into many gorges—scars of earthquake shocks, and sabre-cuts of time. Gorge on gorge, cañon intersecting cañon, pitching down toward the rapid Klamat—a black and boundless forest till it touches the very tide of the sea, a hundred miles to the west.

From Mount Shasta to the Stars.

THE largest and brightest stars, it seems to me, hang about and above Mount Shasta in those cold, bright winter nights of the north. They seem as large as California lilies; they flash and flare, and sparkle and dart their little spangles; they lessen and enlarge, and seem to make signs, and talk and understand each other, in their beautiful blue home, that seems in the winter time so near the summit of the mountain. The Indians say that it is quite possible to step from this mountain to the stars. They say that their fathers have done so often. They lay so many great achievements to their fathers. In this they are very like the white man. But may be, after all, some of their fathers have gone from this mountain-top to the stars. Who knows?

Be Your Own Disciple.

I DARE say any man can date his manhood from some event, from some little circumstance that seemed to invest him with a sort of majesty, and dignify him, in his own estimation, at least, with manhood. A man must first be his own disciple. If he does not first believe himself a man, he may be very sure the world, not one man or woman of the world, will believe it.

The Winter Storm Broken.

THE thunder boomed away to the west one night as if it had been the trump of resurrection; a rain set in, and the next morning Humbug Creek, as if it had heard a Gabriel blow, had risen and was rushing toward the Klamat and calling to the sea. Some birds were out, squirrels had left the rocks and were running up and down the pines, and places where the snow had melted off, and left brown burrs and quills and little shells. The backbone of the winter storm was broken.

The Real Hero.

THE great hero is born of the bitter struggle. Who cannot go down to battle with banners, with trumps and the tramp of horses? Who cannot fight for a day in a line of a thousand strong with the eyes of the world upon him? But the man who fights a moral battle, coolly, quietly, patiently and alone, with no one to applaud or approve, as the strife goes on through all the weary year, and after all to have no reward but that of his own conscience, the calm delight of a duty well performed, is God's own hero. He is knighted and ennobled there, when the fight is won, and he wears thenceforth the spurs of gold, and an armor of invulnerable steel.

Snow in the Sierras.

SNOW! Snow! Snow! The stream that had lain all day in state, in its shroud of frost and fairy-work, was buried now, and, beside the grave, the alder and yew along the bank bent their heads and drooped their limbs in sad and beautiful regret; a patient, silent sorrow! Over across from the cabin the mountain side shot up at an angle almost frightful to look upon, till it lost its pine-covered summit in the clouds, and lay now a slanting sheet of snow. The trees had surrendered to the snow. They no longer shook their sable plumes, or tossed their heads at all. Their limbs reached out no more triumphant in the storm, but drooped and hung in silence at their sides—quiet, patient, orderly as soldiers in a line, with grounded arms. Back of us the same scene was lifted to the clouds. Snow! Snow! Snow! nothing but snow! To right and to left, up and down the buried stream, were cabins covered with snow, white and cold as tombs and stones of marble in a churchyard.

And still the snow came down steadily and white, in flakes like feathers. It did not blow or bluster about as if it wanted to assert itself. It seemed as if it already had absolute control; rather like a king who knows that all must and will bow down before him. Steady and still, strong and stealthy, it came upon us and possessed the earth. Not even a bird was heard to chirp, or a squirrel to chatter or protest. High overhead, in the clouds as it seemed, or rather back of us, a little on the steep and stupendous mountain, it is true a coyote lifted his nose to the snow, and called out dolefully; but that, maybe, was a call to his mate across the cañon, in the clouds on the hill-top opposite. That was all that could be heard.

The Bald-headed Man.

You can nearly always detect a bald-headed man, even while his hat is on his head, by the display and luxuriance of the hair peeping out from under his hat. With the bald-headed man every hair is brought into requisition, every hair is brushed and bristled up into a sort of barricade against the eyes of the curious. The few hairs seemed to be marshalled up for a fierce bayonet charge against any one who dares suspect that the head, which they keep sentry round, is bald. That man is bald and he feels it. Only bald-headed men make this display of what hair they have left.

Spring Disrobing Winter.

The sun came up at last and he let go his hold upon the stream, took off his stamp from pick, and pan, and tom, and sluice, and cradle, and crept in silence into the shade of trees and up the mountain side against the snow. And now Spring came back with a double force and strength. She planted California lilies, fair and bright as stars, tall as little flag-staffs, along the mountain side, and up against the Winter's barricade of snow, and proclaimed possession absolute through her messengers, the birds, and we were very glad. Paquita gathered blossoms in the sun, threw her long hair back, and bounded like a fawn along the hills. Klamat took his club and knife, drew his robe only the closer about him in the sun, and went out gloomy and sombre in the mountains. Sometimes he would be gone all night.

At last the baffled Winter abandoned even the wall that lay between us and the outer world, and drew off all his forces to Mount Shasta. He retreated above the timber line, but he retreated not an inch beyond. There he sat down with all his strength. He planted his white and snowy tent upon this everlasting fortress, and laughed at the world below him. Sometimes he would send a foray down, and even in midsummer, to this day he plucks an ear of corn, a peach, or an apricot, for a hundred miles around his battlement, whenever he may choose.

The Showy Rich Man.

YOUR ostentatious, prosperous man, your showy rich man of America, is so very, very poor, that you do not care to call him your neighbor. It is true he has horses and houses and land and gold, but these horses and houses and land and coins are all in the world he has. When he dies these will all remain, and the world will lose nothing whatever. His death will not make even a ripple in the tide of life. His family, whom he has taught to worship gold, will forget him in their new estates. In their hearts they will be glad that he has gone. They will barter and haggle with the stone-cutter toiling for his bread, and for a starve-to-death price, they will lift a marble shaft above his head with an iron fence around it—typical, cold and soulless! Poor man, since he took nothing away that one could miss, what a beggar he must have been! The poor and unhappy never heard of him; the world has not lost a thought. Not a note missed, not a word was lost in the grand, sweet song of the universe when he died.

Mouths.

THERE are as many kinds of mouths as there are crimes in the catalogue of sins. There is the mouth for hash!—thick-lipped, coarse and expressionless. * * * Then there is the thin-lipped, sour-apple mouth, sandwiched in between a sharp chin and thin nose. Look out! Then there are mischievous mouths, ruddy and full of fun, that you would like to be on good terms with if you had time. Then there is the rich, full mouth, with dimples dallying and playing about it like ripples in a shade, half sad, half glad—a mouth to love. Such was Paquita's. A rose, but not yet opened; only a bud that in another summer would unfold itself wide to the sun.

The Indian Autumn.

THE mountain streams went foaming down among the boulders between the leaning walls of yew and cedar trees toward the Sacramento. The partridge whistled and called his flock together when the sun went down; the brown pheasants rustled as they ran in strings through the long brown grass, but nothing else was heard. The Indians, always silent, are unusually so in Autumn. The majestic march of the season seems to make them still.

A Thunder-Storm in the Mountains.

LATE one September day it grew intensely sultry; there was a haze in the sky and a circle about the sun. There was not a breath. The perspiration came out and stood on the brow, even as we rested in the shadow of the pines. A singular haze; such a day, it is said, as precedes earthquakes. The black crickets ceased to sing; the striped lizards slid quick as ripples across the rocks, and birds went swift as arrows overhead, but uttered no cry. There was not a sound in the air nor on the earth.

Paquita came rushing down to the claim, pale and excited. She lifted her two hands above her head as she stood on the bank, and called to us to come up from the mine. "Come," she cried, "there will be a storm. The trees will blow and break against each other. There will be a flood, a sea, a river in the mountains. Come!" She swayed her body to and fro, and the trees began to sway above her on the hills, but not a breath had touched the mines.

Then it grew almost dark; we fairly had to feel our way up the ladder. A big drop sank in the water close at hand, splashing audibly; the trees surged above us and began to snap like reeds. There was a roar like the sea—loud, louder. Nearer now the trees began to bend and turn and lick their limbs and trunks, interweave and smite and crush, until their tops were like one great black and boiling sea.

Fast, faster the rain in great warm drops began to strike us in the face, as we miners hastened up the hill to the shelter of the cabin. At the door we turned to look. The darkness of death was upon us; we could hear the groans and the battling of the trees, the howling of the tempest, but all was darkness, blackness, desolation. Lightning cleft the heavens. A sheet of flame—as if the hand of God had thrust out through the dark, and smote the mountain side with a sword of fire.

And then the thunder shook the earth till it trembled, as if Shasta had been shaken loose and broken from its foundation. No one spoke; the lightning lit the cabin like a bonfire. Klamat stood there in the cabin by his club and gun.

Sunrise on Mount Shasta.

DAWN was descending and settling around the head of Shasta in a splendor and a glory that words will never touch. There are some things that are so far beyond the reach of words that it seems like desecration to attempt description. It was not the red of Pekin, not the purple of Tyre, or the yellow of the Barbary coast; but merge all these, mixed and made mellow in a far and tender light—snow and sun, and sun and snow, and stars, and blue and purple skies all blended, all these in a splendid, confused and indescribable glory, suffusing the hoary summit, centering there, gathering there, resting a moment—then radiating, going on to the sea, to broad and burning plains of the south, to the boundless forests of fir in the north, even to the mining camps of Cariboo, and you have a sunrise on the summit of Shasta.

A Funeral in a Mining Camp.

As a rule a funeral in the mines is a mournful thing. It is the saddest and most pitiful spectacle I have ever seen. The contrast of strength and weakness is brought out here in such a way that you must turn aside or weep when you behold it. To see those strong, rough men, long-haired, bearded and brown, rugged and homely-looking, with something of the grizzly in their great, awkward movements, now take up one of their number, straightened in the rough pine box, in his miner's dress, and carry him up, up on the hill in silence—it is sad beyond expression.

He has come a long way, he has journeyed by land or sea for a year, he has toiled and endured, and denied himself all things for some dear object at home, and now after all he must lie down in the forests of the Sierras, and turn on his side and die. No one to kiss him, no one to bless him, and say "good-bye," only as a woman can, and close the weary eyes, and fold the hands in their final rest; and then at the grave, how awkward—how silent! How they would like to look at each other and say something, yet how they hold down their heads, or look away to the horizon, lest they should meet each other's eyes; lest some strong man should see the tears that went silently down from the eyes of another over his beard and on to the leaves.

The Chain of Fortune.

No man leaps full grown into the world. No great plan bursts in full and complete magnificence and at once upon the mind. Nor does any one suddenly become this thing or that. A combination of circumstances, a long chain of reverses that refuses to be broken, carries men far down in the scale of life, without any fault whatever of theirs. A similar but less frequent chain of good fortune lifts others up into the full light of the sun. The world, watching the gladiators from its high seat in the circus, will never reverse its thumb against the successful man.

Paquita.

She was surely lovelier now than ever before; tall, and lithe, and graceful as a mountain lily swayed by the breath of morning. On her face, through the tint of brown, lay the blush and flush of maidenhood, the indescribable sacred something that makes a maiden holy to every man of a manly and chivalrous nature; that makes a man utterly unselfish, and perfectly content to love and be silent, to worship at a distance, as turning to the holy shrine of Mecca, to be still and bide his time; caring not to possess in the low, coarse way that characterizes your common love of to-day, but choosing rather to go to battle for her,—bearing her in his heart through many lands, through storms and death, with only a word of hope, a smile, a wave of the hand from a wall, a kiss blown far, as he mounts his steed below and plunges into the night. That is a love to live for. I say the knights of Spain, bloody as they were, were a noble and a splendid type of men in their way.

The Night.

As the sun went down, broad, blood-red banners ran up to the top of Shasta, and streamed away to the south in hues of gold; streamed and streamed as if to embrace the universe in one great union beneath one banner. Then the night came down as suddenly on the world as the swoop of an eagle.

The Indian Account of the Creation.

THE Indians say the Great Spirit made this mountain first of all. Can you not see how it is? they say. He first pushed down snow and ice from the skies, through a hole which he made in the blue heavens, by turning a stone round and round, till he made this great mountain; then he stepped out of the clouds upon the mountain top, and descended and planted the trees all around by putting his finger on the ground. Simple and sublime!

The sun melted the snow, and the water ran down and nurtured the trees and made the rivers. After that he made the fish for the rivers, out of the small end of his staff. He made the birds by blowing some leaves which he took up from the ground among the trees. After that he made the beasts out of the remainder of his stick, but made the grizzly bear out of the big end, and made him master over all the others. He made the grizzly so strong that he feared him himself, and would have to go up on the top of the mountain out of sight of the forest to sleep at night, lest the grizzly, who, as will be seen, was much more strong and cunning then than now, should assail him in his sleep. Afterward the Great Spirit, wishing to remain on earth, and make the sea and some more land, he converted Mount Shasta by a great deal of labor into a wigwam, and built a fire in the centre of it, and made it a pleasant home. After that his family came down and they all have lived in the mountain ever since.

The Association of the Dead.

DEAD men are even more gregarious than the living. No one lies down to rest long at a time alone, even in the wildest parts of the Pacific. The dead will come, if his place of rest be not hidden utterly, sooner or later, and even in the wildest places will find him out, and one by one lie down around him.

Sunset on Mt. Shasta.

THE kingly sun, as if it were the last sweet office on earth that day, reached out a shining hand to Shasta, laid it on his head till it became a halo of gold and glory, withdrew it then, and let the shadowy curtains of night come down, and it was dark almost in a moment.

Climbing the Mountain.

It was perfectly splendid. We were playing spider and fly in the heavens. Down at the mountain's base and pressed to the foamy rim of the river, stood the madroño and manzanita, light, but trim-limbed, like sycamore ; and up a little way were oak, and ash, and poplar trees, yellow as the autumn frosts could paint them ; and as the eye ascended the steep and stupendous mountain that stood over across the river against us, yet so close at hand, the fir and tamarack grew dense and dark, with only now and then a clump of yellow trees like islands set in a sea of green.

Here and there a scarlet maple blazed like the burning bush, and, to a mind careless of appropriate figures, might have suggested Jacob's kine, or coat of many colors. How we flew and dashed around the rocky spurs! Some chipmunks dusted down the road and across the track, and now and then perched on a limb in easy pistol-shot; a splendid gray squirrel looked at us under his bushy tail, and barked and chattered undisturbed; but we saw no other game. In a country famous for its bears, we saw not so much as a track. Down under us on the river bank the smoke of a solitary wigwam curled lazily up through the trees, and the Indian, who stood on the rocks spearing the Autumn run of salmon, looked no taller than a span.

The Death of Paquita.

When I had strength to rise, I went up the warm grassy river bank, peering through the tules in an almost hopeless search for my companions. Nothing was to be seen. The troops on the other bank had gone away, not knowing, perhaps not caring what they had done. The deep, blue river gave no sign of the tragedy now. All was as still as the tomb. I stole close and slowly along the bank. I felt a desolation that was new and dreadful in its awful solemnity. The bluff of the river hung in basaltic columns, a thousand feet above my head; only a narrow little strip of grass, and tules, and reeds, and willows, nodding, dipping, dripping, in the swift, strong river. Not a bird flew over, not a cricket called from out the long grass. "Ah! what an ending is this!" I said, and sat down in despair. My eyes were riveted on the river. Up and down on the other side, everywhere I scanned with Indian eyes for even a sign of life, for friend or foe. Nothing but the bubble and gurgle of the waters, the nodding, dipping, dripping of the reeds, the willows and the tules.

If earth has any place more solemn, more solitary, more awful than the banks of a strong, deep river, rushing, at night-fall, through a mountain forest, where even the birds have forgotten to sing, or the katydid to call from the grass, I know not where it is.

I stole further up the bank; and there, almost at my feet, a little face was lifted as if rising from the water into mine.

Blood was flowing from her mouth, and she could not speak. Her naked arms were reached out, and holding on to the grassy bank, but she could not draw her body from the water. I put my arms about her, and, with a sudden and singular strength, lifted her up and back to some warm, dry rocks, and there sat down with the dying girl in my arms.

She was bleeding from many wounds. Her whole body seemed to be covered with blood as I drew her from the water. Blood spreads with water over a warm body in streams and seams, and at such a time a body seems to be covered with a sheet of crimson.

Paquita!

I entreated her to speak. I called to her, but she could not answer. The desolation and solitude was now only the more dreadful. My voice came back in strange echoes from the basalt bluffs, and that was all the answer I ever had.

The Indian girl lay dead in my arms. Blood on my hands, blood on my clothes, and blood on the grass and stones.

The lonely July night was soft and sultry. The great white moon rose up and rolled along the heavens, and sifted through the boughs that lifted above and reached from the hanging cliff, and fell in lines and spangles across the face and form of my dead.

Paquita!

Once so alone in the awful presence of death, I became terrified. My heart and soul were strung to such a tension, it became intolerable. I would have started up and fled. But where could I have fled, even had I had the strength to fly? I bent my head, and tried to hide my face.

Paquita dead!

Our lives had first run together in currents of blood on the snow, in persecution, ruin and destruction; in the shadows and in the desolation of death; and so now they separated forever.

Paquita dead!

We had starved together; stood by the sounding cataracts, threaded the forests, roamed by the river banks together; grown from childhood, as it were, together. But now she had gone away, crossed the dark and mystic river alone, and left me to make the rest of the journey with strangers and without a friend.

Paquita!

Why, we had watched the great sunland, like some mighty navigator sailing the blue seas of heaven, on the flashing summit of Shasta; had seen him come with lifted sword and shield, and take possession of the continent of darkness; had watched him in the twilight marshal his forces there for the last great struggle with the shadows, creeping like evil spirits through the woods, and, like the red man, make a last grand battle there for his old dominions. We had seen him fall and die at last with all the snow-peak crimsoned in his blood.

No more now. Paquita, the child of nature, the sunbeam of the forest, the star that had seen so little of light, lay wrapped in darkness. Paquita lay cold and lifeless in my arms.

That night my life widened and widened away till it touched and took in the shores of death. . . .

Tenderly at last I laid her down, and moved about. Glad of something to do, I gathered fallen branches, decayed wood, and dry, dead reeds, and built a ready pyre.

I struck flints together, made a fire, and when the surf of light again broke in across the eastern wall, I lifted her up, laid her tenderly on the pyre, composed her face and laid her little hands across her breast. I lighted the grass and tules. So the fire took hold, and leaped, and laughed, and crackled, and reached, as if to salute the solemn boughs, that bent and waved from the cliffs above, as bending and looking into a grave. I gathered white stones and laid a circle around the embers. How rank and tall the grass is growing above her ashes now! The stones have settled and settled, till almost sunk in the earth, but this girl is not forgotten. This is the monument I raise above her ashes and her faithful life.

THE SHIP IN THE DESERT.

WRITTEN in Rome and on the shores of Lake Como in 1874. Published by Chapman & Hall, London, 1874, and Roberts Bros., Boston, 1875. The design of the poem—the book contains one only—is to portray the vastness, the almost *boundlessness* of "the great American Desert,"—the regions between the Mississippi River and the Rocky Mountains. "An infinite sense of *room*." The poet has expressed the belief that this will outlive everything else he has written, simply from its grand subject.

O weary days of weary blue,
Without one changing breath, without
One single cloud-ship sailing through
The blue seas bending round about
In one unbroken blotless hue.

The sunlights of a sunlit land,
A land of fruit, of flowers, and
A land of love and calm delight;
A land where night is not like night,
And noon is but a name for rest,
And love for love is reckoned best.

The Old Sea-King.

GRAND old Neptune in the prow,
Gray-hair'd and white with touch of time,
Yet strong as in his middle prime;
A grizzed king, I see him now,
With beard as blown by wind of seas,
And wild and white as white sea-storm,
Stand up, turn suddenly, look back
Along the low boat's wrinkled track,
Then fold his mantle round a form
Broad-built as any Hercules,
And so sit silently.
Beside
The grim old sea-king sits his bride,
A sunland blossom, rudely torn
From tropic forests, to be worn
Above as stern a breast as e'er
Stood king at sea or anywhere.

On the River.

HER hair pour'd down like darkling wine,
The black men lean'd, a sullen line,
The bent oars kept a steady song,
And all the beams of bright sunshine
That touch'd the waters wild and strong,
Fell drifting down and out of sight
Like fallen leaves, and it was night.

The Sea-King's Bride.

A GREAT, sad beauty, in whose eyes
Lay all the loves of Paradise.

O had you loved her sitting there,
Half hidden in her loosen'd hair:
Why, you had loved her for her eyes,
Their large and melancholy look
Of tenderness, and well mistook
Their love for light of Paradise.

Yea, loved her for her large dark eyes;
Yea, loved her for her brow's soft brown ;
Her hand as light as heaven's bars;
Yea, loved her for her mouth. Her mouth
Was roses gather'd from the south,
The warm south side of Paradise,
And breathed upon and handed down,
By angels on a stair of stars.

Her mouth ! 'twas Egypt's mouth of old,
Push'd out and pouting full and bold
With simple beauty where she sat.
Why, you had said, on seeing her,
This creature came from out the dim
Far centuries, beyond the rim
Of Time's remotest reach or stir.
And he who wrought Semiramis
And shaped the Sibyls, seeing this,
Had bow'd and made a shrine thereat,
And all his life had worshipp'd her,
Devout as north-Nile worshipper.

A Great Soul.

A MAN whose soul was mightier far
Than his great self, and surged and fell
About himself as heaving seas,
Lift up and lash, and boom, and swell
Above some solitary bar
That bursts through blown Samoa's sea,
And wreck and toss eternally.

Spring.

THE black-eyed bushy squirrels ran
Like shadows shatter'd through the boughs;
The gallant robin chirp'd his vows,
The far-off pheasant thrumm'd his fan,
A thousand blackbirds were a-wing
In walnut-top, and it was Spring.

Journeying.

THE clouds of dust, their cloud by day;
Their pillar of unfailing fire
The far north star. And high, and higher . . .
They climb'd so high it seem'd eftsoon
That they must face the falling moon,
That like some flame-lit ruin lay
Thrown down before their weary way.

"Take Men as You Find Them."

AND as to that, I reckon it
But right, but Christian-like and just,
And closer after Christ's own plan,
To take men as you find your man,
To take a soul from God on trust,
A fit man, or yourself unfit:

To take man free from the control
Of man's opinion; take a soul
In its own troubled world, all fair
As you behold it then and there,
Set naked in your sight, alone,
Unnamed, unheralded, unknown:

Yea, take him bravely from the hand
That reach'd him forth from nothingness,
That took his tired soul to keep
All night, then reach'd him out from sleep
And sat him equal in the land;
Sent out from where the angels are,
A soul new-born, without one whit
Of bought or borrow'd character.

The Omaha of the Future.

By pleasant high-built Omaha
I stand. The waves beneath me run
All stain'd and yellow, dark and dun,
And deep as death's sweet mystery,—
A thousand Tibers roll'd in one.
I count on other years. I draw
The curtain from the scenes to be.
I see another Rome. I see
A Cæsar tower in the land,
And take her in his iron hand.
I see a throne, a king, a crown,
A high-built capital thrown down.

In the Desert.

They saw the Silences
Move by and beckon: saw the forms,
The very beards of burly storms,
And heard them talk like sounding seas,
On unnamed heights bleak-blown and brown,
And torn like battlements of Mars;
They saw the darknesses come down
Like curtains loosen'd from the dome
Of God's cathedral, built of stars.

They saw the snowy mountains roll'd
And heaved along the nameless lands
Like mighty billows; saw the gold
Of awful sunsets; saw the blush
Of sudden dawn, and felt the hush
Of heaven when the Day sat down,
And hid his face in dusky hands.

The Red Men's Cemetery.

O BEARDED, stalwart, westmost men,
So tower-like, so Gothic-built!
A kingdom won without the guilt
Of studied battle; that hath been
Your blood's inheritance . . .
Your heirs
Know not your tombs. The great ploughshares
Cleave softly through the mellow loam
Where you have made eternal home
And set no sign.
Your epitaphs
Are writ in furrows. Beauty laughs,
While through the green ways wandering
Beside her love, slow gathering
White starry-hearted May-time blooms
Above your lowly levell'd tombs;
And then below the spotted sky
She stops, she leans, she wonders why
The ground is heaved and broken so,
And why the grasses darker grow
And droop and trail like wounded wing.

Kings in Captivity.

Two sullen bullocks led the line,
Their great eyes shining bright like wine;

Two sullen captive kings were they,
That had in time held herds at bay,
And even now they crush'd the sod
With stolid sense of majesty,
And stately stepp'd and stately trod,
As if 'twere something still to be
Kings even in captivity.

To-morrow.

O THOU to-morrow! Mystery!
O day that ever runs before!
What has thine hidden hand in store
For mine, to-morrow, and for me?
O thou to-morrow! what hast thou
In store to make me bear the now?

O day in which we shall forget
The tangled troubles of to-day!
O day that laughs at duns, at debt!
O day of promises to pay!
O shelter from all present storm!
O day in which we shall reform!

O day of all days for reform!
Convenient day of promises!
Hold back the shadow of the storm.
O bless'd to-morrow! Chiefest friend,
Let not thy mystery be less,
But lead us blindfold to the end.

The Sun at Noon-day.

IT molten hung
Like some great central burner swung
From lofty beams with golden bars
In sacristy set round with stars.

Solemn Silence.

THE solemn silence of that plain,
Where unmanned tempests ride and reign,
It awes and it possesses you,
'Tis, oh! so eloquent.
The blue
And bended skies seem built for it,
With rounded roof all fashioned fit,
And frescoed clouds, quaint-wrought and true;
While all else seems so far, so vain,
An idle tale but illy told,
Before this land so lone and old.

Its story is of God alone,
For man has lived and gone away,
And left but little heaps of stone,
And all seems some long yesterday.

Dead.

Lo! all things moving must go by.
The sea lies dead. Behold, this land
Sits desolate in dust beside
His snow-white, seamless shroud of sand;
The very clouds have wept and died,
And only God is in the sky.

The Land of the Future.

A LAND from out whose depths shall rise
The new-time prophets.
Yea, the land
From out whose awful depths shall come,
All clad in skins, with dusty feet,

A man fresh from his Maker's hand,
A singer singing oversweet,
A charmer charming very wise;
And then all men shall not be dumb.

Nay, not be dumb, for he shall say,
"Take heed, for I prepare the way
For weary feet."
Lo! from this land
Of Jordan's streams and sea-wash'd sand,
The Christ shall come when next the race
Of man shall look upon his face.

Busy Bees.

How sweet the grasses at my feet!
The smell of clover oversweet.
I heard the hum of bees. The bloom
Of clover-tops and cherry-trees
Were being rifled by the bees,
And these were building in a tomb.

Africa.

Behold!
The Sphinx is Africa. The bond
Of silence is upon her.
Old
And white with tombs and rent and shorn;
With raiment wet with tears, and torn,
And trampled on, yet all untamed;
All naked now, yet not ashamed,—
The mistress of the young world's prime,
Whose obelisks still laugh at Time,
And lift to heaven her fair name,
Sleeps satisfied upon her fame.

Beyond the Sphinx, and still beyond,
Beyond the tawny desert-tomb
Of Time; beyond tradition, loom
And lift ghost-like from out the gloom
Her thousand cities, battle-torn,
And gray with story and with time.
Her very ruins are sublime,
Her thrones with mosses overborne
Make velvets for the feet of Time.

The Antelope.

THE large-eyed antelope came down
From off their windy hills, and blew
Their whistles as they wandered through
The open groves of watered wood;
Then came as light as if a-wing,
And reached their noses wet and brown,
And stamped their little feet, and stood
Close up before them wondering.

The Dead African.

AGAIN the still moon rose and stood
Above the dim, dark belt of wood,
Above the buttes, above the snow,
And bent a sad, sweet face below.

She reach'd along the level plain
Her long, white fingers. Then again
She reach'd, she touch'd the snowy sands,
Then reach'd far out until she touch'd
A heap that lay with doubled hands,
Reach'd from its sable self, and clutch'd
With death.

O tenderly
That black, that dead and hollow face
Was kiss'd at midnight. . . .
What if I say
The long, white moonbeams reaching there,
Caressing idle hands of clay,
And resting on the wrinkled hair
And great lips push'd in sullen pout,
Were God's own fingers reaching out
From heaven to that lonesome place?

Solitude.

Lo! date had lost all reckoning,
And Time had long forgotten all
In this lost land, and no new thing,
Or old could anywise befall,
Or morrows, or a yesterday,
For Time went by the other way.
The ages have not any course
Across this untrack'd waste.
The sky
Wears here one blue, unbending hue,
The heavens one unchanging mood.
The far still stars they filter through
The heavens, falling bright and bold
Against the sands as beams of gold.
The wide, white moon forgets her force;
The very sun rides round and high,
As if to shun this solitude.

Misunderstood Souls.

Ah! there be souls none understand;
Like clouds, they cannot touch the land,
Drive as they may by field or town.

Then we look wise at this and frown,
And we cry, "Fool," and cry, "Take hold
Of earth, and fashion gods of gold."

Unanchor'd ships, they blow and blow,
Sail to and fro, and then go down
In unknown seas that none shall know,
Without one ripple of renown.
Poor drifting dreamers sailing by,
They seem to only live to die.

Call these not fools; the test of worth
Is not the hold you have of earth.
Lo! there be gentlest souls sea-blown
That know not any harbor known.
Now it may be the reason is
They touch on fairer shores than this.

The Little Isle.

It lies a little isle mid land,
An island in a sea of sand;
With reedy waters and the balm
Of an eternal summer air.
Some blowy pines toss tall and fair;
And there are grasses long and strong,
And tropic fruits that never fail:
The Manzinetta pulp, the palm,
The prickly pear, with all the song
Of summer birds.
And there the quail
Makes nest, and you may hear her call
All day from out the chaparral
A land where white man never trod,
And Morgan seems some demi-god.

A Lifted Face.

A FACE that lifted up; sweet face
That was so like a life begun,
That rose for me a rising sun
Above the bended seven hills
Of dead and risen old new Rome.

Not that I deem'd she loved me. Nay,
I dared not even dream of that.
I only say I knew her; say
She ever sat before me, sat
All still and voiceless as love is,
And ever look'd so fair, divine,
Her hush'd, vehement soul fill'd mine,
And overflowed with Runic bliss,
And made itself a part of this.

To the Missouri.

O SOUNDING, swift Missouri, born
Of Rocky Mountains, and begot
On bed of snow at birth of morn,
Of thunder-storms and elements
That reign where puny man comes not,
With fountain-head in fields of gold,
And wide arms twining wood and wold,
And everlasting snowy tents,—
I hail you from the Orients.

Shall I return to you once more?
Shall take occasion by the throat
And thrill with wild Æolian note?
Shall sit and sing by your deep shore?
Shall shape a reed and pipe of yore
And wake old melodies made new,
And thrill thine leaf-land through and through?

Three Babes.

THREE mute brown babes of hers; and they—
O, they were beautiful as sleep,
Or death below the troubled deep.
And on the parting lips of these
Red corals of the silent seas,
Sweet birds, the everlasting seal
Of silence that the God has set
On this dead island, sits for aye.

I would forget, yet not forget
Their helpless eloquence. They creep
Somehow into my heart, and keep
One bleak, cold corner, jewel set.

Dark-Eyed Ina.

O DARK-EYED Ina! All the years
Brought her but solitude and tears.
Lo! ever looking out she stood
Adown the wave, adown the wood,
Adown the strong stream to the south,
Sad-faced and sorrowful. Her mouth
Push'd out so pitiful. Her eyes
Fill'd full of sorrow and surprise.

Men say that looking from her place
A love would sometimes light her face,
As if sweet recollections stirr'd
Her heart and broke its loneliness,
Like far sweet songs that come to us,
So soft, so sweet, they are not heard,
So far, so faint, they fill the air,
A fragrance filling anywhere.

And wasting all her summer years,
That utter'd only through her tears,
The seasons went, and still she stood
Forever watching down the wood.

Unnamed Giants.

A RACE of unnamed giants these,
That move like gods among the trees,
So stern, so stubborn-brow'd and slow,
With strength of black-maned buffalo,
And each man notable and tall,
A kingly and unconscious Saul,
A sort of sullen Hercules.

A star stood large and white a-west,
Then Time uprose and testified;
They push'd the mailèd wood aside,
They toss'd the forest like a toy,
That great forgotten race of men,
The boldest band that yet has been
Together since the siege of Troy,
And followed it . . . and found their rest.

Dead Azteckee.

WHITE Azteckee! Dead Azteckee!
Vast sepulchre of buried sea!
What dim ghosts hover on thy rim,
What stately-manner'd shadows swim
Along thy gleaming waste of sands
And shoreless limits of dead lands?

Dread Azteckee! Dead Azteckee!
White place of ghosts, give up thy dead:
Give back to Time thy buried hosts!

The new world's tawny Ishmaelite,
The roving tent-born Shoshonee,
Who shuns thy shores as death, at night,
Because thou art so white, so dread,
Because thou art so ghostly white,
Because thou hast thy buried hosts,
Has named thy shores "the place of ghosts."

Thy white uncertain sands are white
With bones of thy unburied dead
That will not perish from the sight.
They drown but perish not,—ah me!
What dread unsightly sights are spread
Along this lonesome dried-up sea.

White Azteckee, give up to me
Of all thy prison'd dead but one,
That now lies bleaching in the sun,
To tell what strange allurements lie
Within this dried-up oldest sea,
To tempt men to its heart and die.

Old, hoar, and dried-up sea! so old!
So strewn with wealth, so sown with gold!
Yea, thou art old and hoary white
With time, and ruin of all things;
And on thy lonesome borders Night
Sits brooding as with wounded wings.

The winds that toss'd thy waves and blew
Across thy breast the blowing sail,
And cheer'd the hearts of cheering crew
From farther seas, no more prevail.

Thy white-wall'd cities all lie prone,
With but a pyramid, a stone,
Set head and foot in sands to tell
The tired stranger where they fell.

The Boundless Space.

THEY climb'd the rock-built breasts of earth,
The Titan-fronted, blowy steeps
That cradled Time . . . Where Freedom keeps
Her flag of white blown stars unfurl'd,
They turn'd about, they saw the birth
Of sudden dawn upon the world;
Again they gazed; they saw the face
Of God, and named it boundless space.

Famishing.

IT was a sight! A slim dog slid
White-mouth'd and still along the sand,
The pleading picture of distress.
He stopp'd, leap'd up to lick a hand,
A hard black hand that sudden chid
Him back and check'd his tenderness;
But when the black man turn'd his head
His poor mute friend had fallen dead.

The very air hung white with heat,
And white, and fair and far away
A lifted, shining snow-shaft lay
As if to mock their mad retreat.

The Little Maid.

ONE little maid of ten,—such eyes,
So large and lonely, so divine,—
Such pouting lips, such peachy cheek,—
Did lift her perfect eyes to mine,
Until our souls did touch and speak;
Stood by me all that perfect day,
Yet not one sweet word could she say.

She turned her melancholy eyes
So constant to my own, that I
Forgot the going clouds, the sky,
Found fellowship, took bread and wine,
And so her little soul and mine
Stood very near together there.
And O, I found her very fair.
Yet not one soft word could she say;
What did she think of all that day?

The One Lost Birdling.

THIS isle is all their own. No more
The flight by day, the watch by night.
Dark Ina twines about the door
The scarlet blooms, the blossoms white,
And winds red berries in her hair,
And never knows the name of care.

She has a thousand birds; they blow
In rainbow clouds, in clouds of snow;
The birds take berries from her hand;
They come and go at her command.

She has a thousand pretty birds,
That sing her summer songs all day;
Small black-hoofed antelope in herds,
And squirrels bushy-tail'd and gray,
With round and sparkling eyes of pink,
And cunning-faced as you can think.

She has a thousand busy birds;
And is she happy in her isle,
With all her feathered friends and herds?
For when has Morgan seen her smile?

She has a thousand cunning birds,
They would build nestings in her hair;
She has brown antelope in herds;
She never knows the name of care;
Why then is she not happy there?

All patiently she bears her part;
She has a thousand birdlings there,
These birds they would build in her hair;
But not one bird builds in her heart.

She has a thousand birds; yet she
Would give ten thousand cheerfully,
All bright of plume and loud of tongue,
And sweet as ever trilled or sung,
For one small fluttered bird to come
And sit within her heart, though dumb.

She has a thousand birds; yet one
Is lost, and, lo! she is undone.
She sighs sometimes. She looks away,
And yet she does not weep or say.

She has a thousand birds. The skies
Are fashioned for her paradise;
A very queen of fairy land,
With all earth's fruitage at command,
And yet she does not lift her eyes.
She sits upon the water's brink
As mournful soul'd as you can think.

She has a thousand birds; and yet
She will look downward, nor forget
The fluttered white-winged turtle-dove,
The changeful-throated birdling, love,
That came, that sang through tropic trees,
Then flew for aye across the seas.

The waters kiss her feet; above
Her head the trees are blossoming,
And fragrant with eternal spring.
Her birds, her antelope are there,
Her birds they would build in her hair;
She only waits her birdling, love.
She turns, she looks along the plain,
Imploring love to come again.

THE BARONESS OF NEW YORK.

THE last published work of Mr. MILLER, the criticisms on which are too fresh to need supplementary words at the editor's hands. A few journals, like the New York *Evening Mail*, have denounced it as "an outrage," "a monstrosity," etc., but others, whose critics have probably read the work through, admit it possesses some extraordinary beauties as well as bad faults. The plot is more pretentious than that of any preceding poem. The story opens in the far West, and gives to the first part of the book its title, "In the Forest." The heroine next becomes "the Baroness of New York," and the second part is entitled "On Fifth Avenue." The author, at times somewhat in the style of Butler's *Hudibras*, but at other times in his customary cast of verse, hits severe blows at the "Upper Ten" society, so-called, in New York. The opening verses of the book are mainly what constituted the poem read at Dartmouth Commencement, in 1876, which was written at Philadelphia during the Centennial; the remainder of the volume was composed in New York in the Spring and Summer of 1877. Published in September, 1877, by Carleton, New York.

My brave world-builders of the West!
Why, who doth know ye? Who shall know
But I, who on thy peaks of snow
Brake bread the first? Who loves ye best?
Who holds ye still, of more stern worth
Than all proud peoples of the earth?

Yea, I, the rhymer of wild rhymes,
Indifferent of blame or praise,
Still sing of ye, as one who plays
The same shrill air in all strange climes—
The same wild piercing highland air,—
Because, because his heart is there.

The Baroness—In the Wood.

HOW beautiful she was! Why, she
Was inspiration. She was born
To walk God's summer-hills at morn
Nor waste her by a wood-dark sea.
What wonder, then, her soul's white wings
Beat at the bars, like living things?

She ofttime sighed, and wandered through
The sea-bound wood, then stopped and drew
Her hand above her head, and swept
The lonesome sea, and ever kept
Her face to sea, as if she knew
Some day, some near or distant day,
Her destiny should come that way.

How proud she was! How purely fair!
How full of faith, of love and strength!
Her great, proud eyes! Her great hair's length—
Her long, strong, tumbled, careless hair,
Half curled and knotted anywhere,
From brow to breast, from cheek to chin,
For love to trip and tangle in.

How beautiful she was! How wild!
How pure as water-plant this child,
This one wild child of nature, here
Grown tall in shadows! And how near
To God, where no man stood between
Her eyes and scenes no man hath seen.
Stop still, my friend, and do not stir,
Shut close your page and think of her.

How the Night Came.

THE drowned sun sank and died. He lay
In seas of blood. He sinking drew
The gates of heaven sudden to.
Yet long, strong ribbons stretched away
As if the gates still jarred agape—
Tied back by ribbons and red tape.

The tall trees blossomed into stars.
The moon climbed slowly up the cone,
She sat an empress on her throne.
Her silver beams fell down in bars
Between the mighty, mossy trees—
Grand, kingly comrades of the wood,
That shoulder unto shoulder stood
With friendships knit through centuries.

The night came, moving in dim flame,
As lighted by round Autumn sun
Descending through the hazy blue.
It were a gold and amber hue
And all hues blended into one.
The moon spilled fire where she came
And filled the yellow wood with flame.

The Sunset Land.

IN the land of the wonderful sun and weather,
With green under foot and with gold over head,
Where the sun takes flame, and you wonder whether
'Tis an isle of fire in his foamy bed:
Where the ends of the earth they are welding together
In a rough-hewn fashion, in a forge flame red:

In the land where the rabbits dance delicate measures,
At night by the moon in the sharp chapparral:

Where the squirrels build homes in the earth and hoard treasures:
  Where the wolves fight in armies, fight faithful and well;
Fight almost like Christians; fight on and find pleasures
  In strife, like to man turning earth into hell:

Where the plants are as trees: where the trees are as towers
  That toy, as it seems, with the stars at night:
Where the roses are forests: where the wild-wood flowers
  Are dense unto darkness: where, reaching for light,
They spill in your bosom their fragrance in showers
  Like incense spilled down in some sacrament rite.

'Tis the new-finished world; how silent with wonder
  Stand all things around you; the flowers are faint
And lean on your shoulder. You wander on under
  The broad, gnarly boughs, so colossal and quaint,
You breathe the sweet balsam where boughs break asunder—
  The world seems so new, as if smelling of paint.

Fire in the Forest.

THEN suddenly the silent wood
Was sounding like a broken flood,
And far adown some dark smoke curled,
As if from out an under-world.

Slim snakes slid quick from out the grass,
From wood, from fen, from everywhere:
As if they sped pursuing her:
They slid a thousand snakes, and then
You could not step, you would not pass,
And you would hesitate to stir,

Lest in some sudden, hurried tread,
Your foot struck some unbruiséd head.
It was so weird, it seemed withal,
The very grass began to crawl.

They slid in streams into the stream,
They rustled leaves along the wood,
They hissed and rattled as they ran
As if in mockery of man.
It seemed like some infernal dream:
It seemed as they would fill the flood.

They curved and graceful curved across,
Like deep and waving sea-green moss—
There is no art of man can make
A ripple like a running snake.

The wild beasts leaped from out the wood:
They rent the forest as they fled;
They plunged into the foaming flood,
And swam with wild, exalted head.

It seemed as if some mighty hand
Had sudden loosened all command.
They howled as if the hand of God
Pursued and scourged them with a rod.

A Common Code of Men.

His was the common code of men
To pillage, plunder hearts, and then,
Thief-like, depart before the dawn,
And leave behind a haunted hall
With broken statues on the floor—
With household idols scattered o'er,
And only shadows on the wall,
That never, never are withdrawn.

Doughal and the Priest.

THE priest came forth as if he came
From 'twixt twin monarchs of the wood,
That like cathedral columns stood.
And Doughal started. Was he there
To keep his fair maid from despair?
To keep her white, sweet soul from shame?
Had this same priest forever stood
And ever watched him, in this wood?

The silent priest placed hand in hand,
Upheld his cross against the sun,
As in most solemn service done
In any clime or Christian land;
Then, falling on his knees, he prayed
Before the pure and pallid maid,
As to Madonna. Doughal fell
Upon his knees, and all was well.

The Bridal Kiss.

HE careless turned, put forth his hand,
Half stooped as if to heedless kiss
The lips the priest had now made his—
Those lips, the proudest in the land
Had died to touch in that brave time
When valor had a name sublime,—
When Spain's proud banners blew along
The rock-built hills of Jebus, and
A woman's name and woman's fame
Were chorus to the soldier's song.

The Magnet.

THIS child was as Madonna to
The tawny, brawny, lonely few

Who touched her hand and knew her soul.
She drew them, drew them as the pole
Points all things to itself. She drew
Men upward as a moon of spring,
High wheeling, vast and bosomful,
Half clad in clouds and white as wool,
Draws all the strong seas following.

A Majestic Mouth.

How beautiful! How proud and free!
How more than Greek or Tuscan she
In full development. Her mouth
Was majesty itself. Give me
A mouth as warm as summer south—
A great, Greek mouth, for through this gate
Man first must pass to love's estate.

The Forest Aflame.

The flames leapt like some wingéd steed
When furies ride in tempest flight,
They leapt from tossing top and height
Of rosin pine to fragrant fir—
They seemed to lose themselves, to whir
Like sportive birds, and in their speed
Leap on in long advance, and dart
Red lances through the forest's heart.

The birds rose dense, a feathered cloud,
And flew with croakings lorn and loud,
With drooping, weary wings and slow,
And blew toward the cone of snow.
The fierce flame saw them, and he came,
A sounding full red sea of flame.

The winds came like some great, third wave
Across the tossing tops of fire.
The flames leapt high, then high, then higher—
He sounded like some hollowed cave.
Like battle steed, all undismayed,
He leaped like some mad steed. He neighed.
He laughed at clouds of birds. He laid
The forest level where he came.
He fanned the very stars to flame.

Adora in Tears.

A BRIGHT brown nut dropped like a star
From woody heaven overhead,
A wild beast trumpeting afar
Aroused her ere the light had fled.

A stray, dead leaf was in her hair—
Her long, strong, tumbled storm of hair;
Her eyes seemed floating anywhere.
Her proud development, half bare,
And beautiful as chiseled stone
Of famed far Napoli, leaned there
Like some fair Thracian overthrown.

She was not shamed. Her love was high
And pure and fair as heaven's blue.
Her love was passionate, yet true
As upward flame. A stifled sigh
And then a flood of tears, and lo!
A sigh that shook her being so
It startled Doughal where he stood,
Like some bowed monarch of the wood.

Her proud face now fell white as wool,
Her lips fell pale and pityful.
Her great, proud mouth, a splendid flower,
Drooped pale and passionless. Her arms

Reached out in suppliance. Her charms
Like ravished lilies lay. * *
Her soul was beaten as a shore
Is beaten by a storm just o'er
That will but beat and beat the more.

To Fifth Avenue.

O BEAUTIFUL, long, loved Avenue!
So faithless to truth, and yet so true!
Thou camp in battle with the shouts in air,
The neighing of steeds and the trumpet's blare!
Thou iron-faced sphynx; thy steadfast eyes
Encompass all seas. Thy hands likewise
Lay hold on the peaks. The land and the sea
Make tribute alike, and the mystery
Of Time it is thine . . . Say, what art thou
But the scroll of the Past rolled into the Now?

O throbbing and pulsing proud Avenue!
Thou generous robber! Thou more than Tyre!
Thou mistress of pirates! Thou heart of fire!
Thou heart of the world's heart, pulsing to
The bald, white poles. So old; so new.
So nude, yet garmented past desire.
Thou tall splendid woman, I bend to thee;
I love thy majesty, mystery;
Thy touches of sanctity, touches of taint,
So grand as a sinner, so good as a saint.

Thou heaven of lights! I stood at night
Far down by a spire where the stars shot through,
Where commerce throbs strong as a burly sea swell,
And searched the North Star. O Avenue!
If the road up to God were thy long lane of light!—
I lifted my face, looking upward and far
By the path of the Bear, underneath the North Star,

Beyond the gas-lights where the falling stars spin,
And lo! no man can tell, guess he never so well,
Where thy gaslights leave off or the starlights begin.

To Fifth Avenue Again.

O, Avenue, splendid Fifth Avenue!
Thou world in thyself! Thou more than Rome,
When Rome sat throned and preëminent!
Thy spires prick stars in the moon-bound blue
And stand mile-stones on the high road home.
I behold thy strength like a stream's descent
When it flows to the sea filled full to the foam:
My soul it expands as an incense curled,
And proud as a patriot I point the world
To thy achievement and to thine intent.

Dear and delicious, loved Avenue!
I have had my day in the Bois de Bologne,
I have stood very near the first steps of a throne,
I have roamed all the cities of splendor through,
I have masked on the Corso; and many bright nights,
I have dashed Rusk bells down a lane of delights;
On gay Rotten Row I have galloped the rounds,
And, too, have made one of a long line of hounds,
But nothing 'neath sun or tide-guiding moon
Approaches thine populous afternoon.

Adora.

She was dark as Israel; proud and still
As the Lebanon trees on Palatine hill.
She stood as a lone brown palm that grew
In middle desert for the shelter of men
From moving sand and descending flame.
Her name, Adora. Her plain, simple name,

Meant nothing at all until after you
Had seen her face, her presence, and then
From that day forth it had form, and meant
The fairest thing under the firmament.

Her name was as language, and when men knew
No word in all tongues to give utterance to
Their grandest conception of beauty, she
Stood up in their souls, calm, silently,
And filled the blank with her simple name;
And ever at mention or thought of her
Men grew in soul as a growing flame
When dying embers on the altar stir
In the priestess' hands, and all life through
They lived the nobler for the love they knew.

Lost Love.

ALAS! Alas!
Men only count what their fellow has;
They count his gains, but never the cost
Of the jewel, love, that he may have lost.

Your Middle-Men.

I HATE your middle-men; men who
Are ever striving, straining to
A place they don't fit in. They rise,
They hang between the earth and skies,
As hung the prophet's coffin. Lies
Are on their lips, in all their deeds.
Their lives are lies, their hollow creeds
Make infidel, sweet souls that bloom
On humble ground, in lonely gloom.
Write me not of that class. My name,
Thank God, is not of these. I claim

No middle-class or place. I lie
Secure, and shall not fall, for I
Am of the lowliest lot—as low
As God's own sweetest flowers grow.

Go View Fifth Avenue.

The crowded carnival of Rome,
That Saturn crowns each vernal year,
Knows nothing in its proudest day
Like this magnificent display
Of men and maidens moving through
This populous, proud Avenue.
Yea, I have tracked the hemispheres,
Have touched on fairest land that lies
This side the gates of Paradise;
Have ranged the universe for years,
Have read the book of beauty through,
From title-leaf to colophon,
While pleasure turned the leaves.
Yet on
This island bank your bark should strand,
Your feet should cleave this solid land;
That you may live, alone to view
The glory of this Avenue.

Go ye, and wander if you will,
For grace in far-off countries. Still,
When every foreign land is trod,
I know ye will return, and you
Will lift your hands, protesting there
Was never yet a scene so fair
This side the golden gates of God.

On Rousseau's Isle, Geneva.

I do remember long ago,
A boy, by Leman's languid flow,

Alone, alone! God, how alone!
To land and language all unknown.
I strolled so wearily and slow,
And sad as after death. The crowd
Was gay, and populous, and loud.

Alone and sad I sat me down
To rest on Rousseau's narrow Isle,
Below Geneva. Mile on mile,
And set with many a shining town,
Tow'rd Dent du Midi danced the wave
Beneath the moon.

Winds went and came,
And fanned the stars into a flame.
I heard the loved lake, dark and deep,
Rise up and talk as in its sleep.
I heard the laughing waters lave
And lap against the farther shore,
An idle oar, and nothing more,
Save that the Isle had voice, and save
That round about its base of stone
There plashed and flashed the foamy Rhone.

The star-set Alps they sang a tune
Unheard by any soul save mine.
Mont Blanc, as lone and as divine
And white, seemed mated to the moon.

The past was mine, strong-voiced and vast:
Stern Calvin, strange Voltaire, and Tell,
And two whose names are known too well
To name, in grand procession passed.

The Farewell Letter.

FAREWELL! God help me now. For such
Hard conflicts tide about my heart
That I do hesitate.

The part
Of man is in the ranks to die
Hard battling for the shining right;
But when all things partake a touch
Of darkness and a touch of light,
The skein comes tangled. Then the woof
And warp of life proves reason-proof.
O heaven! for a sword so true
Of edge that I might cleave this through!

The years lift like a stair. Arise
And climb the stairway to the skies,
And look possession of the world,
That lies quite conquered at your feet.
Yet range not far, I do entreat;
Black clouds will cross the fairest skies,
The fullest tides must ebb and flow;
The proudest king that e'er unfurled
His banner, met his overthrow

Farewell, farewell! for aye, farewell.
Yet must I end as I began.
I love you, love you, love but you—
I love you now as never man
Has loved since man and woman fell,
Or God gave man inheritance,
Or sense of love, or any sense.
And that is why, O love, I can
Lift up to you my burning brow
To-night, and so renounce you now.

The Morning After the Storm.

THE morning must succeed the night.
All storms subside. The clouds drive by.
And when again the glorious light
From heaven's gate comes bursting through,
Behold! the rains have washed the sky
As bright as heaven's bluest blue.

The White-Girdled Moon.

THE great, white-girdled moon,
As soft as summer afternoon,
Came wheeling up the sea, and lay
Her broad, white shoulders bare as day,
As if at some fair, festal ball
Of gathered stars at Carnival.

Silentness.

O GOLDEN, sacred silentness!
Take thou the silver coin of speech,
And bribe your way to hearts, so less
Than hearts the silences shall reach.

The Worth of the Soul.

THE body is not much. 'Twere best
Take up the soul and leave the rest.
It seems to me the man who leaves
The soul to perish, is as one
Who gathers up the empty sheaves
When all the golden grain is done.

Woman's Instincts.

MEN are not shrewd as women are;
A woman feels an atmosphere,
Sees all, where men see aught at all.
Her instincts lead where reason fall.
Now it may be the reason is,
Her little feet are set more near
The light of golden gates ajar.

Copyists.

I HATE all copyists. My plan
Would be to paint a picture; do
A thing original. Now you
Have room to paint eternity,
In this vast land where scarcely yet
God's rounding compass has been set;
And, for a land so very new,
Your skies are glorious to see.

And yet your silly painters paint
The old Italian figure, saint
And dark Madonna; all outdone
The century they first struck oil.
Paint nature, sir; cast off the coil
Of custom. Why paint mortal more,
Where God leads ever on before,
As visible as your broad sun?
Ah no! Your feeble painters paint
Their imitation, till the taint
Of felony attaches.

The Earth a Level Ball.

I HATE astronomers, the fools
That spin the stars by iron rules,
And make this level earth a ball,
That tumbles like a bumble-bee,
And bumps among the blossomed stars,
Till some fall, loosened by the jars.

O, that the world were what she seems,
A broad, vast, level land of dreams;
A boundless land, a shoreless sea,
A God-encompassed mystery—
With far edge stretching, climbing to
The sapphire walls of fading blue,
That touch on far eternity!

The West's World-Builders.

THESE brave world-builders of the West,
They came from God knows where, the best
And worst of four parts of the world.
With naked blade, with flag unfurled,
They bore new empires in their plan.
A motley band; the bearded man,
The eager and ambitious boy,
The fugitive from fallen Troy,
The man of fortune, letters, fame,
The old-world knight with stainless name,
The man with heritage of shame.

The thriftless Esaus, hairy men
Who roamed and tracked the trackless wood,
Good, if it pleased them to be good,
Or cruel as some wild beast when
He tears a hunter limb by limb,
And so sits gloating over him.

Then cunning Jacobs, crafty men,
With spotted herds, who loved to keep
Along the hills a thousand sheep,
Who strove with men and strove as when
The many sons digged down a wall
And gloried in their fellows' fall.

Then black-eyed pirates of the sea,
That sailing came from none knew where,
That sought deep wooded inlets there,
And took possession silently;
To rest, they said, in loved repose—
To rest or rob, God only knows.

I only know that when that land
Lay thick with peril, and lay far
It seemed as some sea-fallen star,

The weak men never reached a hand
Or sought us out that primal day,
And cowards did not come that way.

A Sad White Dove.

O! I DID know a sad white dove
That died for some sufficient love—
Some high-born soul with wings to soar,
That stood up equal in his place,
That looked her level in the face,
Nor wearied her with leaning o'er,
To lift him where she lonely trod,
In sad delights the hills of God.

Fair as Young Junos.

THEY were fair as young Junos. Bright gold shone in bar,
And diamonds flashed thick as the meadow sown dew,
That mirrors the gold of the morn-minted star.

The Halo.

ONE still, soft summer afternoon
In middle deep of wood, the two,
Where tangled vines twined through and through,
Together sat upon the tomb
Of perished pine, that once had stood
The tall-plumed monarch of the wood.
The far-off pheasant thummed a tune,
The faint far billows beat a rune
Like heart regrets. The sombre gloom
Was ominous. Around her head
There shone a halo. Men have said
'Twas from the dash of Titian hue

That flooded all her storm of hair
In gold and glory. But they knew,
Yea all men know there ever grew
A halo round about her head
Like sunlight scarcely vanishéd.

Thank God, He's Dead.

HER two clasped hands fell down.
Her face forgot its dark, fierce frown,
And sad and slow she shook her head.
O, if, indeed, it were but hate!
But love and hate do intertwine,
A serpent, and a laden vine.
But where is Doughal?
He is dead!
Thank God, the man is dead! and I
Am free as any maid to wed.
And if he be not dead, what then?
Do I not hate him with a hate
That will not let me hesitate
Now at the last?
Above all men
I hate this cursed, cold man who fled,
And left me in the flame to die . . . .
And he is dead, thank God, is dead!

Should I Desert Him?

We two once stood
On peril's bristled height alone;
We two, in God's high-lifted light,
Exulting but in purity.
Shall I desert him overthrown?
Forsake my friend because his soul
Is slimed and perishing?

Ah, me!
'Twere base to fly and leave a friend
All bleeding on the battle-field,
Without one shelt'ring hand or shield
To help when battle's thunders roll.

But that were little. Dying there
In glory's front, with trumpet's blare,
And battle's shout blent wild about—
The sense of sacrifice, the roar
Of war, the soul might well leap out—
The snow-white soul leap boldly out
The door of wounds, and up the stair
Of heaven to God's open door,
While yet the hands were bent in prayer.
But ah! to leave a soul o'erthrown,
And doomed to slowly die alone!

Near, Yet Far.

His soul was as some ship that drew
All silent through the burst of seas,
Pursuing some far distant star,
That spun unfixed forever through
The boundless upper seas of blue.
She seemed so near, and yet so far.
Just now she seemed as near as woe;
Just now she seemed as far as though
They dwelt in the antipodes.

SONGS OF ITALY.

THIS work is in press at the time of this writing, but the kindness of the author has placed its proof-sheets at our disposal. It consists of 56 poems, mostly written in Italy from 1872 to 1874, and dated from Florence, Venice, Rome, Naples, Como, Ancona, Turin, Pestam, and other places. Some have been published in *Scribner*, the *Independent*, and other American magazines and journals; others are new. The "Song of the Centennial," originally contributed to Frank Leslie's *Illustrated Weekly*, is printed at the close of the volume. To be published by Roberts Bros., Boston.

This land it is desolate, dead as death!
Never the sound of a beast or a bird,
Nor voices of Nature above a breath;
Never the wild deer's quick retreat,
Never the pheasant's far drum-beat,
Only the tiresome talk of the brook,
Only the tourist holding a book,
A red-bound book as a lamp for his feet!

Rome.

SOME levelled hills, a wall, a dome,
That lords its gilded arch and lies,
While at its base a beggar cries
For bread, and dies,—and that is Rome.

Yet Rome is Rome ; and Rome she must
And shall remain beside her gates,
And tribute take of kings and States,
Until the stars have fallen to dust.

Yea, Time on yon campagnian plain
Has pitched in siege his battle tents;
And round about her battlements
Has marched and trumpeted in vain.

These skies are Rome ! The very loam
Lifts up and speaks in Roman pride;
And Time outfaced and still defied
Sits by and wags his beard at Rome.

A Falling Star.

LIKE a signal light through the night let down
A far star fell through the dim profound,
As a jewel that slipped God's hand to the ground.

Why Nights were Made.

THE nights they were made to show the light
Of the stars in heaven, tho' storms are near.

Christmas Time in Venice.

THE high-born, beautiful snow came down,
Silent and soft as the terrible feet
Of Time on the mosses of ruins. Sweet
Was the Christmas time in the watery town.
'Twas a kind of carnival swelled the sea
Of Venice that night, and canal and quay
Were alive with humanity. Men and maid
Glad in their revel and masquerade,
Moved through the feathery snow in the night,
And shook black locks as they laughed outright.

Morn in Venice.

Some sounds blow in from the distant land;
The bells strike sharp, and as out of tune,
Some sudden, short notes. To the east and afar,
And up from the sea, is lifting a star
As large, my beautiful child, and as white
And as lovely to see as your little white hand.
The people have melted away with the night,
And not one gondola frets the lagoon.
See! Away to the east—'tis the face of morn—
Hear! Away to the west—'tis the fisherman's horn.

The Kiss of Faith.

CHILD of the street, I will kiss you! Yea,
I will fold you and hold you close to my breast.
And as you lie resting in your first rest,
And as night is pushed back from the face of day,
I will push your tumbled and long, strong hair
Well back from your face, and kiss you where

Your ruffian, bearded, black men of crime
Have stung you and stained you a thousand time;
And call you my sister, sweet child, as you sleep,
And waken you not, lest you wake but to weep.

Yea, tenderly kiss you. And I shall not be
Ashamed, nor stained in the least, sweet dove,—
Tenderly kiss, with the kiss of Love,
And of Faith and of Hope and of Charity.
Nay, I shall be purer and better then;
For, child of the street, you, living or dead,
Stained to the brows, are purer to me
Ten thousand times than the world of men,
Who but reach you a hand to lead you astray. . .
But the dawn is upon us! Rise, go your way.

To a Waif of the Street.

If we two were dead, and laid side by side
Right here on the pavement, this very day,
Here under the lion and over the sea,
Where the morn flows in like a rosy tide,
And the sweet Madonna that stands in the moon,
With her crown of stars just across the lagoon,
Should come and should look upon you and me,—
Do you reckon, my child, that she would decide,
As men do decide and as women do say,
That you are so dreadful, and turn away?

If the angel were sent to choose to-day
Between us two as we lay here,
Dead and alone in this desolate place,—
You, white with a hunger and stained with a tear,
Or I, the rover the whole world through,
Restless and stormy as any sea,—

If the angel were sent to choose, I say,
This very moment the best of the two,
Looking us two right straight in the face,
Child of the street, he would not choose me.

The fresh sun is falling on turret and tower,
The far sun is flashing on spire and dome,
The marbles of Venice are bursting to flower,
The marbles of Venice are flower and foam:
Child of the street, oh, waken you now!
There! bear my kiss on your brave white brow,
Through earth to heaven: and when we meet
Beyond the waters, poor waif of the street,
Why, then I shall know you, my sad, sweet dove,
And claim you and kiss you with the kiss of love.

Sunrise in Venice.

THE east is blossoming! Yea, a rose,
Vast as the heavens, soft as a kiss,
Sweet as the presence of woman is,
Rises and reaches, and widens and grows
Large and luminous up from the sea
And out of the sea, as a blossoming tree.

Richer and richer, so higher and higher,
Deeper and deeper it takes its hue;
Brighter and brighter it reaches through
The space of heaven and the place of stars,
Till all is as rich as a rose can be,
And my rose-leaves fall into billows of fire.
Then beams reach upward as arms from a sea;
Then lances and arrows are aimed at me.
Then lances and spangles and spars and bars
Are broken and shivered and strown on the sea;
And around and about me tower and spire
Start from the billows like tongues of fire.

Lone.

I AM as lone as lost winds on the height;
As lone as yonder leaning moon at night,
That climbs, like some sad, noiseless-footed nun,
Far up against the steep and starry height,
As if on holy mission. Yea, as one
That knows no ark, or isle, or resting-place,
Or chronicle of time, or wheeling sun,
I drive forever on through endless space.
Like some lone bird in everlasting flight,
My lonesome soul sails on through lonesome seas of
night.

A Storm in Venice.

THE pent sea throbbed as if racked with pain.
Some black clouds rose and suddenly rode
Right into the town. The thunder strode
As a giant striding from star to star,
Then turned upon earth and franticly came,
Shaking the hollow heaven. And far
And near red lightning in ribbon and skein
Did write upon heaven Jehovah's name.
Then lightnings went weaving like shuttle-cocks,
Weaving black raiment of clouds for death;
The mute doves flew to Saint Mark in flocks,
And men stood leaning with gathered breath.
Black gondolas flew as never before,
And drew like crocodiles upon the shore;
And vessels at sea stood further at sea,
And seamen hauled with a bended knee.
Then canvas came down to left and to right;
And ships stood stripped as if stripped for fight!

The Ideal.

I STOOD by the lion of St. Mark in that hour
Of Venice, when gold of the sunset is rolled
From cloud to cathedral, to turret and tower,
In matchless, magnificent garment of gold.
Then I knew she was near; yet I had not known
Her form or her face since the stars were sown.

We two had been parted—God pity us!—when
The stars were unnamed and all heaven was dim;
We two had been parted far back on the rim
And the outermost border of heaven's red bars;
We two had been parted ere the meeting of men,
Or God had set compass on spaces as yet;
We two had been parted ere God had set
His finger to spinning the purple with stars,—
And now, at the last in the gold and set
Of the sun of Venice, we two had met.

* * * *

Then, my love she is rich! My love she is fair!
Is she pure as the snow on the Alps over there?
She is gorgeous with wealth! "Thank God, she has bread,"
I said to myself. Then I humbled my head
In gratitude. Then I questioned me where
Was her palace, her parents? What name did she bear?
What mortal on earth came nearest her heart?
Who touched the small hand till it thrilled to a smart?
'Twas her year to be young. She was proud, she was fair—
Was she pure as the snow on the Alps over there?

And the Real.

I TOLD her all things. Her brow took a frown;
Her grand Titian beauty, so tall, so serene,

The one perfect woman, mine own idol queen!
Her proud swelling bosom it broke up and down:
Then she spake, and she shook in her soul as she said
With her small hands upheld to her bent, aching
head,
"Go back to the world! go back and alone,
Thou strange, stormy soul, intense as mine own!"
I said: "I will wait! I will wait in the pass
Of death, until Time he shall break his glass!

* * * *

"It is breaking my heart; but, 'tis best," she said.
"Thank God that this life is but a day's span,
But a wayside inn for weary, worn man—
A night and a day; and, to-morrow, the spell
Of darkness is broken. Now, darling, farewell!
Nay, touch not the hem of my robe!—it is red
With sin that your own sex heaped on my head!
But go, love, go! Yet remember this plan,
That whoever dies first is to sit down and wait
Inside death's door, and watch at the gate."

Longing for Home.

I MISS, how wholly I miss my wood,
My matchless, magnificent, dark-leaved fir,
That climbs up the terrible heights of Hood,
Where only the breath of white heaven stirs!
These Alps they are barren; wrapped in storms,
Formless masses of Titan forms,
They loom like ruins of a grandeur gone,
And lonesome as death to look upon.

O God! once more in my life to hear
The voice of a wood that is loud and alive,
That stirs with its being like a vast bee-hive!
And oh! once more in my life to see

The great bright eyes of the antlered deer;
To sing with the birds that sing for me,
To tread where only the red man trod,
To say no word, but listen to God!

To the American Flag.

You stars stand sentry at the door of dawn.
You bars break empires. Kings in vain
Shall rave and thunder at Freedom's fane,
Till the stars leave heaven and the bars be gone.
Then wave, O flag, like the waves of the sea·
Yea, curve as the waves curve, wild and free,
And cover the world. Exult in the sun,
But thunder and threaten where the black storms run;
And the years shall be yours while the eons roll;
Ay, yours till the heavens be rolled as a scroll.

MISCELLANIES.

THE ONE FAIR WOMAN, THE BLUE AND THE GREY, AND MINOR WRITINGS.

"THE One Fair Woman" is a most curious romance, with strong tinges of reality, founded upon the author's visits to Italy. Some of the sketches of travel with which it abounds were contributed to the New York *Independent*, the *Overland Monthly*, and *Gentleman's Magazine*. They were to have appeared in book form as simply notes of Italian journeys, but, by suggestion, the story was inwoven with them. The work was hardly a success, because tedious; but as a guide-book to Italy it will be found to be an improvement on some others of more practical pretensions. The verse on the opposite page, from Swinburne, may have suggested the title. Published by Chapman & Hall, London, 1874, in four volumes, and by Carleton, New York, in 1874, in one volume.

"The Blue and the Grey" is a story written for the *Cincinnati Enquirer* and subsequently revised for and published in *The Somerset Gazette*, Somerville, N. J. It is sufficiently voluminous for a volume.

The poetical selections are from the poems "Custer and his Three Hundred," "The Inauguration of President Hayes," and "The Sioux Chief's Daughter." A few also are interspersed from "The First Fam'lies of the Sierras."

There lived a singer in France of old,
By the tideless, dolorous, midland sea.
In a land of sand and ruin and gold
There shone one woman and none but she.
And finding life for her love's sake fail,
Being fain to see her, he bade set sail,
Touched land, and saw her as life grew cold,
And praised God seeing; and so died he!

—SWINBURNE.

The Eternal City.

THE sun goes down on Rome; and round about Rome on the mighty mountain tops was drawn a girdle of fire. Twenty miles away to the west, as they returned, flashed the sea in the dying sun of Italy, like a hemisphere of flame. Before them, in the middle of the great Campagna, with its far off wall of eternal and snowy mountains, huddled together the white houses of Rome, like a flock of goats gathered to rest for the night; and mighty St. Peter's towered above them all like a tall shepherd keeping watch and ward. "Now I can see that it was no chance or accident that built the Eternal City in the centre of this mighty amphitheatre," said Murietta. "Nature ordered it. She pointed to the little group of hills lifting out of the plain by the Tiber and said, 'Build your city on the Palatine!'"

Italy Tired.

ITALY looks so very tired. Let her lie down and rest. She is old and weary, and worn, and storm-stained, and battered, and battle-torn, till it seems like irreverence to ask her now to rise up and take a place among the powers of the earth. Let her rest, and we will respect, aye, reverence her still. We will come up from the under-world, and sit at her feet and listen, and learn from her songs of a thousand years.

Lake Como.

PEACE, and the perfect summer. Cool waters, and music all the time floating on the waters from under the banners of strange lands. People coming and going away. Beautiful Saxon women, and tall half Greek fishermen. Citizens sitting in the cool of the trees by the water. Clouds blowing against the blue sky. White snow peaks flashing afar off in the sun. Fruit at your hand and flowers at your feet. Peace in the air. Comeliness everywhere. This is Como.

Poets.

SUCCESSFUL men live in the age in which they are born. Great men live in advance of it. Poets and painters belong to no age. They fit in nowhere on the top of the earth. They are more out of place than the other great men in the world's gallery of statuary. Strange, restless, and unhappy men, they hasten on through life, forgetting that the end of the road is but a grave. But the gods love them; and this must be their consolation, for certainly they have little else.

Faces Change.

FACES change so. Let a face be backed by blood and mettle, let the soul be hallowed by experience, and made mellow as a ploughed field by furrows that have torn it up; let it be made charitable of the sins of others by a sense of its own sins,—and you have a face that will wear as many changes of expression as the wind and weather.

A Suggestion.

WHEN a man returns late at night and kisses his wife with more than ordinary tenderness, she may be pretty certain that he has been in mischief.

A Perfect Face.

It was a splendid, dark, dreamy face. It seemed to move before you, to pass on, to look back, to lead you. It beckoned from, and belonged to the future. It was of a race that you might imagine, but would never find, though you should go the whole girdle of the earth. It was the divinest face that had ever belonged to woman since the blessed Madonna. Standing before it, as it looked back over its shoulders from the cloud and mystery from the future, you would have to say this face is as the face of woman will be millions of ages in the years to come, when we have attained to perfection on earth.

Do Not Drift.

You had better sail boldly on in almost any direction than drift without any direction at all. You had better sail in the maddest storm that ever troubled your sea of life, than lie on the sea and drift with any wind that chooses to blow.

The Little Hand.

There was a pretty beggar-boy, with his feet in sandals fastened with red silk ribbons, a sheepskin coat, and a red shirt open in the breast, and the prettiest face that could be. How well he played! His head would drop to one side, his pretty lips pout out, his great, brown eyes half hiding under his hair that had been a fortune to a belle of fashion; and such a perfect pathos! And then his little dimpled brown hands would not reach out at all; it was a timid hand, half hiding behind the little woolly sheepskin coat, with its rows of brass buttons, its stripes, its braids, and its trinkets about the breast and over the shoulders—a hand full of dimples, and dirty, too, no doubt, but the shyest and sweetest little hand that ever reached out and touched any man's heart and opened his pocket, took out all the pennies, and made the man glad to give them.

A Picture.

THE moon kept climbing and climbing, and peeping in and peering over, till it looked right straight down on the group of gathered worshippers kneeling under the shadow of the great black cross, and made a picture that any man might remember, to carry with him around the world, hang on the walls of his heart, and wear it there! And though fire and flood might sweep away all that he possessed in the world, still that picture would remain and rest and refresh its possessor, whenever he chose to open his heart and look in again.

More than Beautiful.

How beautiful she was! Ah, how more than beautiful! The rose and sea-shell color of her face and neck, the soft baby complexion, the sweet surprise on her face, the old expression of inquiry and longing, the lips pushed out and pouting full and as longing for love, the mouth half open as if to ask you the way into some great brave heart, where she could enter in and sit down and rest, as in some sacred temple.

Be Silent and Let God Speak.

How few people have the good sense to sit silent in the carriage as they drive through the groves, and let God speak!

None Utterly Bad.

No man is utterly bad. Set this down as one of the great truths which the world does not understand at all. Every man has a great deal of good in his heart; every man on earth has this. Only in some it is so far, so very far hidden away that we never can find it. It was waiting the resurrection. It is the bit of gold in the bottom of the mine, away down in the dark bottom.

Honor.

WERE you to ask me what I deemed the first requisite to happiness, I would answer: A high sense of honor! Were you to ask me what I deemed the three things necessary to make a perfect man, I should answer: In the first place, honor; in the second place, *honor;* in the third place, HONOR!

Were I a lecturer, a minister, a public speaker of any kind, I would make it my mission to teach this one lesson, and this alone, to America. Alas! That which made Greece the marvel of the earth may now be counted as among the lost arts. You take lessons in French, in art, literature—a thousand things; but that high sense of honor, man's obligations to man, is forgotten. That highest of all philosophy which Socrates taught is now never thought of.

Love of the Beautiful.

IF you were not born with an appreciation, a worship of the beautiful, then go and learn it, as you learn mathematics, language, philosophy; study it every day—when you walk, when you ride, when you rest by the roadside. The flight of a bird gracefully drooping, curving, whirling through the air; the shape and tint of a single autumn leaf; the movement and the voice of the wind in the forest; a deep, rolling river between its leaning banks of trees; the sweet, curled moon in the heavens; the still, far stars; the movement of a proud, pure woman as she walks, the graceful lift of her little foot, the dimpled hand, the delicious, rounded wrist, the proud development, the lifted face, the lovely lifted face as it looks into space for God. Oh! if you love not these, I pity you; indeed I do.

If you were to ask me where I thought the greatest happiness was to be found—I mean pure, sweet and inexpressible delight—I should say: in the love of the beautiful.

If you will take the pains to consider this a moment—and you ought to give it years of consideration—you will find that all things are beautiful, or trying to be beautiful; the whole earth, all things on the earth or in the sea; everything is struggling, all the time, for some expression of beauty. The law of the beautiful is as general and as absolute as the law of gravitation. You may drop the vilest piece of earth on the roadside as you pass by. You come along next year and you will find it is giving some expression of beauty in little flowers, tall, strange weeds, or moss that lifts a thousand perfect spangles from out its velvet carpet.

Yet you cannot come to love the beautiful in a day. The worship of Nature is sweet. But Nature is a jealous God. You shall not rush into her temples with soiled hands and benumbed soul, and rest and be glad. She will cast you out if you attempt it. You must take off your shoes as you enter the Mosque of Constantinople, and bow your head and be silent. How much more glorious are the temples of Nature? Democratic as she is, she must have at least something of the respect you pay to the temples of man. You must pass into her temple by degrees. Why, it is a half life's journey to her heart from the outer door, where you must leave your shoes as you enter.

Reputation.

You must keep your record of honor only with yourself and your God. The testimony of your neighbor about yourself will not satisfy your own conscience at all. Reputation is hardly the kind of testimony, I think, that is used in the Court of the Eternal. Newspaper paragraphs are not evidence in courts of law or equity, even on earth. Do not expect them to be evidence in heaven.

I believe that men have gone straight from the gallows to God with the whole world howling condemnation at their heels. I believe that men have died with the reputation of saints, and yet have groaned in their souls as they died, deceived the world even in death, and have gone straight to the abode of the damned.

Baby-world.

There must be in the vast and incomprehensible system of stars one star further away than all others—one star on the outermost edge—one farthest star on which the tired imagination might sit and look beyond, and see only the open void and vacant blue. But astronomists say not.

Did ever you try to fix and define the outer and the utmost limit of memory? Try it. It is amusing, to say the least. Baby-world is the wonder world. You remember your first word; the first step you took, perhaps. Your big brother's complaints and your sweet mother's praise; your first pants; and it is just possible that away back there among the ruins of the dead years you may in a day of singular clearness positively stumble over your own cradle. It is like finding a new wall under old Troy. And then the beautiful, blushing girls that came trooping in upon you all the time in that tender age. And how they did muss you, and fuss over you, and kiss you every day, till you cried out with suffocation. But, alas! now that you are in no danger of suffocation, they come not any more. Surely we were nearer heaven then than now.

General Custer.

WHEN the world stood dumb with wonder,
When the land lay torn asunder,
And the smoke of battle's thunder
Rolled from out the rift and rents,
Wreathing, wrapping battle-tents,
Where the giants march and muster,
Mounting columns, regiments,
Through the battle's storm and bluster
Rose and rode the gentle Custer.

"Where is Custer?" came the cry,
When men met to do or die,
Where is Custer? Cannon's rattle
From the blazing bank of battle,
Booming, booming, answer back,
"Lo! afront the rush and rattle,
Riding down Death's battle-track,
Sword in hand, and hair blown back,
Lo! a boy leads men to battle!"

The long strong grasses bend the head
In patient pity o'er the dead—
In brother's pity for the brave
Three hundred in their Spartan grave—
In mother's pity for the true
And country-loving, tawny Sioux,
Perchance in ghostland once again
They meet along the lawless plain,
And rove with driving winds and rain.

O Custer and thy comrades, where
Have ye pitched tent in fields of air
Above the Rocky Mountain's brow,
In everlasting glory now?
Ye shine like some high shaft of light,
Ye march above the bounds of night,
And some stray singer yet shall rise
And lift your glory to the skies
In some grand song of wild delight.

The Capitol at Washington.

GRANITE and marble and granite!
Corridor, column and dome.
A Capitol, huge as a planet,
And mighty as marble-built Rome!

Stair-steps of granite to glory!
Go up, with thy face to the sun;
They are stained with the footsteps and story
Of giants and battles well won.

True Merit.

No man need stilt himself up, or seek applause, or friends in high places, or loud praise. If he belongs to the front he will get there in time, and will remain there when he arrives.

Noses.

SMALL noses are a failure. This is the verdict of history. Give me a man, or woman either, with a big nose—not a nose of flesh, or a loose flabby nose like a camel's lips; not a thin, starved nose that the eyes have crowded out and forced into prominence, but a full, strong, substantial nose, that is willing and able to take the lead; one that asserts itself boldly between the eyes, and reaches up toward the brows, and has room enough to sit down there and be at home. Give me a man, or woman either, with a nose like that, and I will have a nose that will accomplish something. I grant you that such a nose may be a knave; but it is never a coward nor a fool—never.

The New Parnassus.

SOMEWHERE in these Sierras will they name the new Parnassus. The nine sisters, in the far New Day, will have their habitation here, when the gold hunter has gone away, and the last pick lies rusting in the mine. The sea of seas shall rave and knock at the Golden Gate, but this shall be the vine-land, the place of rest, that the old Greeks sought forever to find. This will be the land of eternal afternoon. A land born of storm and rounded into shape by the blows of hardy and enduring men, it shall have its reaction—its rest. The great singer of the future, born of the gleaming snows and the gloomy forests of the Sierras, shall some day swing his harp in the wind and move down these watered and wooded slopes to conquer the world with a song for Peace.

Tears.

TEARS flow as freely for joy as for grief. Between intense delight or deepest sorrow the wall is so thin you can whisper through it and be heard.

A Race for Love and Life.

Two tawny men, tall, brown and thewed
Like antique bronzes rarely seen,
Shot up like flame. She stood between
Like fixed, impassive fortitude.
Then one threw robes with sullen air,
And wound red fox-tails in his hair,
But one with face of proud delight
Entwined a crest of snowy white.

She stood between. She sudden gave
The sign, and each impatient brave
Shot sudden in the sounding wave.
The startled waters gurgled round;
Their stubborn strokes kept sullen sound.

O then awoke the love that slept!
O then her heart beat loud and strong!
O then the proud love pent up long
Broke forth in wail upon the air;
And leaning there she sobbed and wept
With dark face mantled in her hair.

Now side by side the rivals plied,
Yet no man wasted word or breath;
All was as still as stream of death.
Now side by side their strength was tried,
And now they breathless paused and lay
Like brawny wrestlers well at bay.

And now they dived, dived long, and now
The black heads lifted from the foam,
And shook aback the dripping brow,
Then shouldered sudden glances home.
And then with burly front the brow
And bull-like neck shot sharp and blind,
And left a track of foam behind . . .
They near the shore at last; and now

The foam flies spouting from a face
That laughing lifts from out the race.

The race is won, the work is done!
She sees the climbing crest of snow;
She knows her tall, brown Idaho.

www.ingramcontent.com/pod-product-compliance
Lightning Source LLC
LaVergne TN
LVHW011238110826
845150LV00006B/1679

* 9 7 8 1 4 2 5 5 1 3 3 1 3 *